The Complete
Winter Sports
SAFETY MANUAL

Bear Klaw Press
Environmental Guide Series

Volume 1
**California: An Environmental
Atlas and Guide**

Volume 2
**Eating Hearty in the Wilderness with
Absolutely No Cleanup:
A Backpacker's Guide to Good Food
and "Leave No Trace Camping"**

Volume 3
**Winter Fun—Where!
A Guide to ALL the Major Trailheads
in Northern California and Nevada**

Volume 4
**The Complete Winter Sports
Safety Manual**

The Complete Winter Sports

SAFETY MANUAL

Staying Safe and Warm
while
Snowshoeing, Skiing,
Snowboarding,
Snowmobiling, and Camping

With a Special Section on Winter Driving

Bern Kreissman

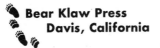
Bear Klaw Press
Davis, California

Library of Congress Card Number: 96-086484
International Standard Book Number: 0-9627489-6-X

Typing of manuscript by Kathy Huntziker, Pages Plus.

Graphic design, typography and page layout production by Jeanne Pietrzak and Jennifer Tomich, Graphic Gold.

Cover design and illustrations by Sue Wilkerson, Your Next Design. Illustrations have been adapted from the following sources: CorelDraw® image package; USDA Forest Service, Pacific Northwest Region; USDA Forest Service, Intermountain Region; USDA Forest Service, U.S. Ski Association Tahoe Nordic Search and Rescue Team; Sacramento Bee research; California Department of Boating and Waterways; Washington State Parks and Recreation Commission.

Index by Teresa L. Jacobsen.

Manufactured in the United States of America
10 9 8 7 6 5 4 3 2 1

Library of Congress Cataloging in Publication Data
Kreissman, Bern
The Complete Winter Sports Safety Manual
Includes index

Bear Klaw Press
926 Plum Lane, Davis, California 95616

Phone: 916-753-7788; Fax: 916-753-7788

For Shirley—Again
Editor, Friend, Loving Companion

Out of this nettle, danger, we pluck this flower, safety.

–Shakespeare

CONTENTS

Introduction ix

1: Winter Safety 3
    Winter Driving 3
    Chain Controls 6
    Road Delays and Closures 6
    Driving in Snow 7
    Driving in Fog 11
    Driving in Rain 11
    Safety Recommendations 12

2: Clothing for Snowshoers, Nordic Skiers, Snow
    Campers 13
        Base Layer 13
        Insulating Layer 14
        Outer Layer 17

3: Gear for Snowshoers, Nordic Skiers,
    Snow Campers 21
        Winter First Aid Kits 25
        Global Positioning Units and
        Telephones 28
        Exercise—Warm Up, Cool Down 29
        Food 31
        Water 33

4: Winter Hazards 37
  Avalanches 37
  Travel On Ice 45
  Hypothermia 46
  Wind Chill 50
  Dehydration 51
  Frostbite 51
  Altitude Sickness 52
  Hyperventilation 53
  Lost or Injured Party 53
  Overdue Party 55
  Back Country Safety 55
  Snowshoe and Nordic Ski Safety
  Rules 56
  Alpine Ski Safety Rules 58
  Snowboard Safety Rules 60
  Sledding Safety Rules 61
5: Snowmobile Safety 63
  Clothing 64
  Safety Equipment 66
  Cold Water Exposure 67
  Winter Hazards 68
  Snowmobile Safety Code 68
  Snowmobile Code of Ethics 69
6: Winter Camping Safety 71
7: First Aid Safety 75
8: Skin Protection 77
  Sunscreens 77
  Insect Repellents 78
9: Eye Protection 81
10: Leave No Trace 85
11: Further Reading 89
Index 93

Introduction

Winter sports have shown a phenomenal growth in popularity in the last several decades. In the '70s and '80s, a bare handful of firms were producing metal/ plastic "high tech" snowshoes. Today more than 70 firms across the country are scrambling to satisfy the increasing demands for these new lightweight 'shoes. Nordic skiing popularity continues an upward spiral, and snowboarding's growing array of participants have pushed that sport into the mainstream of winter recreation. Similarly, snowmobiling now claims more than 10 million active participants.

Producers and promoters have recognized the lure of snow and ice, and are planning new outlets for winter recreation—snow bicycling, ski booting (skiing on boots alone), ski sledding, and snowshoe racing are but a few examples, with other still unknown sports waiting in the wings. Even ice climbing, a practically unknown sport a decade back, is almost commonplace today.

Injuries, even death, are also commonplace among winter recreationists, and with the growth in popularity comes a concomitant rise in crippling hurts and fatalities. Most of these incidents are preventable. Planning and common sense are the handmaids of safety. One

cannot protect a fool from himself, but hopefully, this work will assist most winter sports participants to arrive home safely.

Many people have assisted in the preparation of this volume, but I particularly want to thank Karen Finlayson and her colleagues at the Eldorado National Forest Information Center. The author would appreciate comments and suggestions and may be reached in care of the Press.

Bern Kreissman
January, 1997

Bear Klaw Press
(916) 973-7788
bearklaw@dcn.davis.ca.us

Winter Sports Safety

Winter Safety

Each winter, newspapers, radio and television carry grisly reports of fatal car accidents on iced-over roads, of lost skiers found frozen a stone's throw from warmth and security, of snowshoers overwhelmed and devastated by avalanches they themselves had triggered, and of outdoor revelers in flimsy party clothing suddenly overtaken and ravaged by fierce winter gales. Many of these obituary accounts carry an underlying note of how simply the dreadful denouement might have been avoided if only the victims had prepared properly. Play in the snow can be a glorious adventure, but fickle winter conditions can turn a sunlit day into a whiteout blizzard in a matter of minutes. Tragedy is lying in wait for the uncaring, the unwary, the unprepared.

Winter Driving

Most people realize that the most dangerous part of a winter outing is the drive to and from the resort or trailhead. Driving in winter's cold, wet, snowy, and icy conditions, challenges your car engine to the fullest. To meet such circumstances, your car should be at maximum operating efficiency. Before venturing into snow country, you should make a thorough check of the electrical system (battery, ignition, and lights), brakes, tires, exhaust, heating and cooling systems, and windshield wipers and washers. Be sure your car is winterized.

- **Batteries:** Check for corroded cables and clamps. Clean all connectors with a wire brush and a solution of baking soda and water. Have your battery checked for full charge.
- **Windshield Wipers:** Replace old or damaged wiper blade inserts or any blade that skips or streaks.
- **Cooling System:** Keep the antifreeze level high. Antifreeze should protect to 30 degrees below zero and even more (-40° to -50°) for residents of extremely cold areas.
- **Brake, Power Steering, Automatic Transmission Fluids:** Check all fluid lines and add fluid where necessary.
- **Engine Oil:** Change your oil and filter before winter travel and add fresh oil. Normally multigrade oils, 10W-30 or 10W-40, will allow for easier starting in cold weather. In extremely cold areas 10W-20 is a good choice.
- **Tires:** Check for condition and good tread showing. Check pressure weekly since pressure can drop one pound (per square inch—psi) for every ten degree drop in temperature.
- **Hoses and Belts:** Winter weather is particularly hard on hoses and belts and leads to cracking or fraying. Check for any defects and test the belt tension by pressing down in the center of the belt. If the belt gives more than an inch, it should be replaced or tightened.
- **Create a Winter Driving Kit for the Car:**
  - Tire chains, repair links, and tighteners
  - Ice scraper and/or a commercial de-icer

- Small broom or stiff brush to remove snow from roof, hood, and headlights. Snow left on any of these areas increases the potential for decreased visibility when the car is put in motion
- Large rag or old towel to wipe slush and snow from the lights and mirrors
- Paper towels
- Kitty litter (or sand) for added traction under the drive wheels
- Traction mats for additional traction
- Snow shovel to free the car if it gets snowed in, or to remove snow from under the tires
- Blanket, emergency blanket, and extra warm clothes
- Plastic garbage bags and/or tarpaulin to lie on when applying chains
- Flashlight and extra batteries
- First aid kit (especially for scraped knuckles after you have applied the chains)
- Battery jumper cables
- Tow cable
- Candle lantern and matches
- Portable AM/FM radio and extra battery
- Extra food and water
- Flares
- Car key duplicates (to be carried on your person)
- Toilet paper
- Whistle—three blasts are a call for help
- Knife
- Cellular phone

Large parties and convoys should consider:
- Portable winch
- Chain repair tool
- Stove, fuel, and cooking kit
- Saw
- Reflective signal triangles

Chain Controls

Always carry chains, chain tighteners and repair links. A ground sheet to keep you dry while installing the chains is a convenience. Chain control legislation has been enacted in most states that support winter sports. In most states you must stop and install chains when highway signs indicate that chains are required. A chain control checkpoint will be established about a mile beyond the first "chains required" signs. Be aware that control areas may move rapidly from one point to another because of changing weather or road conditions. When chains are required, wait until you can pull off the highway to the right, completely and safely. Do not stop in a traffic lane; you will put yourself in great danger. Be sure to apply the chains to the drive wheels of your car.

Speed limits are drastically reduced when chains are required, but may be raised if the conditions warrant a higher speed. The appropriate limits are generally posted along the highway. Driving at a higher speed invites a traffic citation and chain and car damage to boot.

When removing chains, pull well beyond the signs reading "end chain control" to an uncongested pull-off area to the right, where you may remove them safely. Avoid those areas where many cars obstruct the highway.

Road Delays and Closures

Weather and road conditions can change rapidly and may occasion a change in chain control points or a closure of the highway. A highway that was open when you drove up may be closed or be under chain restrictions when you start down. Accidents or spinouts, which may block the road for hours, happen frequently during storms. Zero or very low visibility, caused by blowing snow in high winds, also calls for roadway closure. Such closures occur frequently on many major mountain highways in the winter.

Driving in Snow

The most important element in winter driving is the mind-set. Drivers must be aware constantly of road conditions and the traffic about them, and they must drive at speeds appropriate to the weather, road condition, visibility, and traffic. Drivers should be snugly dressed and comfortably seated. Bulky, heavy clothes and gloves should be removed at the first safe opportunity to stop (never struggle out of a coat or a sweater while the car is in motion). Lightweight, non-constricting, warm outerwear, which allows drivers to concentrate on driving, is recommended. A full zipper jacket, a light warm hat, and thin leather gloves are ideal for winter motoring.

Drivers should be seated comfortably in easy reach of the foot pedals, with seat and shoulder belts in place. Adjust your seat so that you can just hang your wrists over the top of the steering wheel when you extend your arms. The head restraint should be close to the head as possible and directly behind (3-4 inches below the top of your head). The best hand position is at 9 o'clock and 3 o'clock, not at the 10 o'clock and 2 o'clock we were formerly taught. Driving experts say the "9-3" set provides maximum control and permits a quick and precise steer to left or right. Easy-on, easy-off sunglasses are a must for winter driving.

Before setting the car in gear, start the engine and turn the heat control to "hot" for two minutes before switching on the defrost button. Preheating will prevent moisture from fogging the inside of the windshield when warm air hits the glass. If the windshield or windows do fog up, open a window a crack, and turn the defroster fan to maximum. Be sure your wipers are off before you start your engine to protect the blades and the wiper motor.

To start a car on ice or snow, make sure there is a clear path for the wheels for several feet—some shoveling may be necessary. Ease out of the parking space without spinning the drive wheels. Keep your front wheels straight and maintain a low speed at a low gear (second or reverse depending on your parking situation). You may need traction assistance with a traction mat, kitty litter, or sand under the drive wheels. If you use such aids, be sure no one is standing in a direct line with the drive wheels. Many a bystander has been hurt by objects thrown up by the drive wheels. Gently rocking the car back and forth with no wheel spinning may allow you to get out of an iced-over patch of the parking lot. Never gun the motor if you get stuck; the spinning wheels will only dig you deeper into the hole. You must use minimum power to keep the wheels from spinning. Many car manuals recommend procedures for rocking a car out of a bad patch.

Always allow extra time for a trip in or out of snow country. Winter trips to the mountains are consistently more time consuming than similar trips in dry weather, so allow for such added time in your travel plans.

Keep your tires fully inflated. An underinflated tire is more likely to skid, particularly on icy or wet roadways. (This recommendation applies equally in summer. Underinflated tires are not safer in hot weather.)

Keep your gas tank as full as possible. One cannot predict serious traffic delays or major detours necessitated by weather, road closures, or accidents. Keep your tank at least half-full to avoid gas line freeze up.

Keep your windshields and windows clear. Wash your car headlights clean. Stop at a safe turnout to brush snow and slush from the glass areas and mirrors.

Do not mix sleeping pills and driving. A nighttime pill can impair morning alertness. Residual effects can last up to 17 hours.

Keep your headlights on in the daytime for added visibility and safety. Tests have shown that daytime running lights have reduced collisions by more than 10%. At dark, protect your night vision. Do not stare at approaching headlights. If oncoming lights strike your eyes, focus on the right shoulder of the road.

Never drive while drowsy. If you are suddenly aware that you are not sure where you are, or if you cannot recall the last several miles of roadway, if your head nods or you jerk awake, if you have difficulty keeping your eyes open and focused, or if your eyes fixate on a particular spot—you are sleepy! Pull over, rest or nap and even consider stopping for the night.

Slow down. Drive at speeds appropriate to prevailing conditions. However, if the speed is reasonable, try to keep up with the flow of traffic. A wide disparity in speeds can be dangerous. Stopping distances are much greater on ice and snow than on dry surfaces, as much as eight times longer, so keep at least twelve car-lengths back of the vehicle before you. Keep your speed low and steady, do not accelerate quickly, and avoid unnecessary turns or lane changes. Try to maintain a straight course, but if you must change lanes, signal for that lane change as you would for a turn. On approaching a hill, take note of other drivers' actions, and stay far enough behind the car immediately ahead so that you may avoid a slowdown or a stop. Sufficient space in front of your car will allow you to maneuver carefully, avoid any stranded vehicle, and change speeds if necessary to carry the car over the crest. On the downhill use low gear to slow down, and stay off the brakes as much as possible to avoid skids. Look far down the road and keep your eyes moving to spot potential problem areas before you reach them. Plan ahead, take note of possible traffic emergencies and plan escape scenarios.

If braking, pump the brakes lightly (but not on a car with antilock brakes!); gentle, slow brake applications (squeeze braking) are recommended by the AAA to avoid locking the wheels and skidding. If you start to skid, do not panic and do not hit the brakes! Turn the front wheels in the direction the rear of the car is skidding. Then easily turn the wheel in the opposite direction to straighten out. To help avoid skids, keep the car moving slowly but steadily. Take curves cautiously, avoid any sudden changes of speed or direction, and stay off the road shoulders and edges.

Watch for icy spots on bridges, overpasses or underpasses, north-facing slopes, and shaded areas. At sundown, be aware of the possibility of black ice on the road from snow melt earlier in the day. Stopping on ice requires particular care. When the temperature is right at or slightly above freezing, 32°F, stopping distances are twice that for stopping at 0°F. The melting snow and ice at 32°F create particularly slick road surfaces. Slow down! AAA recommends squeeze braking with declutching (manual transmission) or shifting to neutral (automatic transmission) along with the "heel and toe" method. "Keep the heel of your foot on the floor and use only your toes to apply firm, steady pressure on the brake pedal just short of lockup, the point at which the wheels stop turning." You must keep your heel on the floor! With antilock brakes on the other hand, "do not pump the pedal or remove your foot from the brake."

AAA also recommends that you not use your parking brake in snow country. Slush can freeze all parts of the brake system and lock the emergency brake. Automatic shift cars should be left with the shift arm in "Park" position, and manual transmission vehicles should park in first gear or reverse. If advisable, chock your wheels. The Automobile Association advises drivers to be sure their "fender wells and exhaust pipes are clear of ice and snow" since frozen slush can trap the front wheels and make steering impossible, and plugged exhaust pipes are dangerous.

Driving in Fog

Since fog is a frequent accompanist of winter weather, special precautions should be taken when driving in reduced visibility circumstances:

- Slow down
- To change lanes or cross traffic, roll down the window to listen for cars you may not be able to see
- Keep your low beam headlights on. Remember to turn them off when parking.
- Keep your windshield clear, use your defroster and windshield wipers if necessary
- If you must stop, pull off the highway as far as possible and step away from your car to a safe zone

Driving in Rain

Driving in a hard rain also limits visibility, and driving precautions as for fog prevail. In a teeming downpour it is smart to stop at a rest area or a protected road zone to wait out the deluge. If you must stop on the highway, pull off the roadway as far as possible. Also, remember that the first ten minutes of a heavy storm are the most dangerous as the rainfall mixes with road-oil and debris to form a slick surface. If the car is stuck in mud, follow all the rules for starting on ice.

Be aware of the potential for hydroplaning—a situation in which the tires lose contact with the road, often resulting in skids. Keep your tires properly inflated and watch for possible hydroplaning circumstances—standing water, rain drops bubbling on the road, or sloshing noises from the tires. At thirty miles per hour, properly inflated tires with good tread will maintain contact with the road. Cars traveling at sixty miles per hour may hydroplane regardless of the merit of the tires. To reduce the chances of hydroplaning, slow down, avoid hard braking or sharp turning, drive in the tracks of the vehicle ahead, and increase the distance to the car immediately ahead of you to at least twelve car-lengths. Slow down in any case. A midsize car on a wet road, driving at 60 miles per hour, needs 280 feet to come to a stop. At 75 miles per hour, 545 feet is required—that's almost two football fields.

Safety Recommendations

Before you go, check road and weather conditions, and be sure that your car and gear are equal to a worst possible scenario situation. All winter sports states provide detailed information regarding weather, road conditions, avalanche potential, snow conditions, traffic and resort area situations. Use those services. Check in with the local ranger station for the very latest information on backcountry snow status, and leave word with them of your contemplated wilderness route. Leave the same word with a responsible party at home:

• Where you are going—leave a marked map
• When you plan to depart
• When you plan to return
• Who you are going with

Clothing for Snowshoers, Nordic Skiers, Snow Campers

The layering system for clothing provides the greatest comfort and warmth with the lightest weight and the fewest garments. With three lightweight layers, a contemporary snowshoer can be warmer and more comfortable than the nineteenth century fur-trapper in a twenty-pound bearskin coat and a five-pound beaver hat. Multiple layers allow snowshoers, Nordic skiers, hikers, or any strenuous winter sports enthusiasts to adjust their attire easily in response to changes in weather and, particularly, body temperature. As snowshoers and Nordic skiers know, body heat fluctuates markedly as they tramp uphill, stop for lunch, run into a rain or snow squall, reach windy peaks, or glissade downhill in deep shade.

Base Layer

Since your body will pump out anywhere from two to four quarts of perspiration on a strenuous trek, the primary function of the base layer is to transport the sweat away from the body; it should also provide warmth.

Underwear and Socks: Synthetic long underwear and lightweight synthetic socks do the job best. Wool is acceptable since it will keep you warm when wet, but it can be heavy, soggy, and itchy, and it is more expensive than synthetics. Treated polyester, polypropylene, and the score of associated variants are the fabrics of choice for the base layer. Cotton, when wet with perspiration, will draw the heat from your body and can kill you. Never, never, never wear cotton underwear.

Synthetic longjohns and shirts generally come in three weights: light, medium, or expedition weight. Wear the weight suitable for the weather conditions and the exertion level of the activity. Light or medium suits are generally best during active periods of an outing. Expedition weight serves best on winter camping excursions or on long stretches of inactivity. Insulated underwear is not a good idea unless you are planning to sit still in the wilderness for lengthy junctures (ice fishing, sleigh riding). Generally, insulated underwear will not transport perspiration effectively, and it prevents the possibility of an easy cool-down when overheated. Thus, it destroys the adaptability of attire required by active outdoor sportspeople.

Gloves: Soft polypropylene glove liners as the first layer on the hands provide the versatility all snow trekkers need—easy adaptability from no protection to light protection to full protection.

Insulating Layer

Socks: Over the soft synthetic sock next to the foot, wear a heavy, cushioning outersock. Currently, any wool, bulky synthetic, or wool synthetic blends are among the most popular outersocks. Rising fast in acceptance, particularly for winter sports enthusiasts, are the flat-seamed fleece socks, such as those made of Polartec 300 by Acorn Products Co. (Lewiston, Maine). These relatively new socks are remarkably warm, breathable, moisture managing, odor resistant, and easy to care for. Polartec seems sure to vie with, and possibly eclipse, wool as the sock fabric of choice in the future.

Another sure bet for future popularity are the waterproof-breathable socks made with a laminate or film such as Gore-Tex. Dupont's "Seal Skinz" may be worn singly as a waterproof outer layer, or the insulated model may be worn as both an insulator and waterproofer. As soon as prices fall to a reasonable range, one may expect to see most snowshoers in lightweight running shoes and waterproof breathable socks.

Boots: Nordic ski boots are required for cross-country skiers, but snowshoers have a choice—a conflicting choice, lightweight or waterproof. Since weight on the foot is onerous in hiking (a common truism holds that one pound on the foot is equal to 5-10 pounds on the back) and even more so in snowshoeing, a snowshoer should opt for the lightest possible boot consistent with day long comfort. Snowshoers out for a lengthy day trip, and snow campers, should choose waterproof boots—particularly snow campers, since wet boots can ice over during the night. Recreational snowshoers may opt for dry feet with waterproof boots (or waterproof socks), neoprene over-the-shoe booties, or even lightweight rubbers. Avid snowshoe racers eschew even the over-the-shoe booties and make their races in the lightest possible supportive canvas, or leather running shoes. A gimmick to consider for a short day's outing is to encase the socked foot in a plastic bag (the bag goes between the outer sock and the shoe). Though your socks will be wet with perspiration at the day's end, your feet will have remained warm throughout the course of a short day's tramp.

Pants: Non-constricting pants of dense wool, or synthetic pile or fleece make for an excellent insulating layer. Some snowshoers opt for expedition weight synthetic longjohns for the second level. Knickers of wool or fleece are also popular for winter sports. Deep, strong pockets with some form of closure are more than a convenience for winter sportspeople, and a sturdy belt is an advisable accessory.

Shirt/Sweater: Wool or a heavy synthetic shirt, and a light fleece sweater (100-200 weight) are ideal for one-day trippers. A thick pile or fleece hooded jacket (300 weight), or even better, a down jacket with attached hood, is recommended for snow campers. All insulating garments should be simple to don or remove, and the successive layers should not add any restrictions to easy movement.

Neck Gaiter: Polypropylene or fleece neck warmers double and triple as hats, earmuffs, or even balaclavas. Thin silk or polypropylene neck gaiters can provide an extra layer of warmth under a hat or hood in severe weather. Silk balaclavas also serve in that capacity.

Hat: A warm, brimmed, ear protective hat of wool, felt, synthetic fleece, or insulated fabric is an absolute must in the winter wild. Since up to seventy percent of body heat may be dissipated by a bare head, lost skiers have died for want of a hat. For full sun protection, a brim is essential in snow country unless you are wearing totally enclosed goggles. A second lightweight tennis hat or a visor is strongly advised for those periods of activity when the going is hot. A balaclava is comforting during cold snaps and in snow camps. A second warm hat is advisable for snow campers.

Gloves: Over the glove liners, an array of insulating gloves are available—wool (particularly boiled wool), insulated water-resistant leather (leather gloves are difficult to waterproof fully), and fleece in a variety of synthetics. The choice is personal, but do not buy gloves which do not dry easily and/or do not keep your hands warm when wet. Fingerless gloves are useful when equipment repair is called for or for close work around camp. One way to beat the high cost of camping is to buy inexpensive garden or work gloves and cut off the fingertips to whatever length suits you best. Wool or fleece gloves should have rubber, leather, or leather-like strips or dots on the palms for good gripability. Mittens are warmer than gloves.

Outer Layer

Gaiters: Waterproof gaiters should cover the leg from the lowest shoelace on your boot to the knee. Gaiters should be easy on-easy off, and should have some tightening device at the top to ensure "stay-up" over the course of a strenuous day. Mini-gaiters (low gaiters) may look cute but they do little good in heavy snow. For really frigid weather, insulated gaiters are available.

Pants: Windproof/waterproof pants which pass perspiration through but keep rain out (waterproof/breathable) are markedly superior to waterproof non-breathable fabrics. Snowshoers and skiers work up a full sweat on the trail and need garments which will transport perspiration out from the body. Coated nylon materials will keep the rain out, but after a full day in the snow such garments will be dripping with sweat.

Choose pants which go on or off easily over boots. Many pants with short zippers or snap arrangements will go on (or off) over shoes, but only after a tussle. For the sake of tranquillity and composure, avoid such garments. Good pants should have extra protection at abrasion-prone areas. If one can swallow the price tag, a rainproof breathable pair of pants with a full zipper (top to bottom) is a great convenience on the trail, and covered, closeable pockets are another useful feature.

Jackets: Breathable rainproof jackets are an even great requisite than their accompanying pants. The torso is particularly vulnerable to cold and consequent hypothermia, and must be protected. The jacket should be large enough to accommodate the insulating clothing, and long enough to cover well below the belt line. The jacket should be long enough to resist riding up under a backpack. A full-length zipper for easy on/off, and fully protected outside pockets as well as sturdy inside storage pockets are the mark of a well designed jacket. An attached hood is a must, preferably one that provides full vision with full protection.

Non-breathable waterproof jackets, such as polyurethane coated nylon, will do an excellent job of keeping the rain out, but wearers should anticipate a heavy sweat buildup inside the jacket—enough to saturate the insulating layer below.

Hats: The waterproof hood on the jacket serves best as the outside layer for the head. However, many hats are designed to act as both the insulating layer and the windproof shell. If you carry only one such hat, however, you lose versatility in dress. The best advice is to carry a lightweight balaclava (as the base layer in cold weather), a warm hat with a brim sufficient to shield the eyes, a lightweight, brimmed tennis hat for eye protection during the sweaty stretches and, as mentioned, the hood of your jacket as it may be needed.

Gloves: Nylon, quick-drying shells, either gloves or mittens, or waterproof breathable mittens provide the requisite outer cover for the hands. Many shell-type fabrics may be made near-waterproof with brush on solutions such as those by Aqua-seal or Nikwax. Gloves take a beating in normal wear and should be made of abrasion resistant fabrics with palms designed to grip metal tools, and other such smooth equipment.

All winter garments should be designed to accommodate the next underlayer easily, with no extra bulk or bagginess. Constricting clothes impede both insulation and movement and should be rejected—shun any and all Spandex!

Gear for Snowshoers, Nordic Skiers, Snow Campers

In addition to the equipment normally carried by hikers or backpackers, winter sports groups should carry gear designed specifically for snow and cold weather emergencies. Most of these items should be carried by each member of the party, but, at discretion, some items may be distributed at less than one for every trekker.

- **Map(s) and Compass:** Snow hikers, snowshoers, or Nordic skiers must be particularly adept in their ability to lay out a route devoid of trail markers and to find the way home.
- **Special Tape:** To supplement the map and compass, highly visible, fluorescent-like, pink or yellow survey tape can be tied to tree branches along a route to

expedite the way back. It can also serve as a signal communications device among groups split off from the main party—"We went that-a-way." If you use survey tape, be sure to remove every strip on the return trip.

• **Snow Shovel:** In an actual test, a group of skiers was assembled to excavate a one cubic meter (35 cubic feet) hole in a mound of fresh avalanche debris. They first dug using only hands, skis, and poles; the average time was 45 minutes. The second time they dug with a shovel; the average time, 8 minutes—five times faster! Moral: make sure you have a snow shovel on your winter hikes. Excellent lightweight, aluminum, Lexan, or other polycarbonate shovels are available. Almost all the shovels collapse for ease in carrying. A typical plastic shovel weighs less than 24 ounces.

• **Snow Probe:** Collapsible probe poles, ten to twelve feet long when extended, are recommended for backcountry snow trekkers, particularly for groups headed for avalanche territory. Some snowshoe or ski poles are designed with removable grips and baskets. When snapped or screwed together, depending on the model, a set of these poles acts as a probe.

• **First Aid Kit:** A good backpacking first aid kit, supplemented by elastic tape for sprained ankles; heat packs for hands, feet, and body; glucose for prevention or treatment of hypothermia; electrolytes for rehydration; and waterproof/windproof matches is advised for the backcountry snow hiker. Several companies make good first aid kits, and Atwater Carey (Boulder, Colorado) makes customized kits for particular sports, and provides their "Walkabout Kit," supplemented as noted, customized for snowshoers, Nordic skiers, and snow campers.

- **Multiple Purpose Tool:** A single lightweight tool with pliers, screwdrivers, file, knives, and other implements is basic insurance for snow trips. The Leatherman Survival Tool is one of the most imitated instruments on the market, but its quality is unsurpassed, except, perhaps, by the Leatherman Super Tool which provides two additional tools and several more functions. The smallest member of this elegant family is the Mini-Tool (with pliers also), far better than a pocket knife for each member of the group.

- **Emergency Blanket:** For one day trips, the two-ounce Space Emergency Blanket (56″ x 84″ aluminized sheet), originally developed as a super insulator for NASA, is a recommended choice. For longer trips, the more versatile (groundsheet, tarp, sunshade, water-proof cover, blanket) ten-ounce All Weather Blanket (56″ x 81″ four-layer, aluminum sheet and fabric backing between plastic film leaves) should be considered. Both blankets act to reflect up to 80% of radiated body heat back to the body. When cold and fatigued, the blanket should be worn, metallic side in, over the head, with legs drawn up to the chest in a fetal position, to conserve as much body heat as possible. In case of an accident, after caring for any possible wound, wrap the patient in the blanket to help prevent post trauma shock. Both blankets reflect radar, and may be used for emergency signaling.

- **Duct Tape:** The everything remedy, from foot blisters to broken ski poles. It deserves its reputation as the required *vade mecum* of the outdoors. Never enter the woods without it. Strapping tape is also useful for a variety of quick repair situations.

- **Candles:** Long-burning candles are recommended. Some trekkers prefer canned heat such as "Cook n' Heat" or a multiple wick candle such as Newick. The wicks sit in a lidded metal can of paraffin, and may be moved and lit singly for illumination, or doubly or triply for heat and cooking.

- **Metal Cup:** A one-pint cup with folding handles that can sit right over a flame is the choice for winter snow outings. Some of these cups come with lids, which help speed the snow-to-boiled-water process. Note: Never eat snow or ice when fatigued. Melting snow in the mouth requires more energy than your body can afford, and it cools the body internally. Drink lots of water. High energy exercise creates a perspiration loss of two to four quarts in a day, and failure to replace that loss results in extreme fatigue.

- **Signal Mirror:** It is claimed that a signal mirror flash can be seen as much as 100 miles away. Whatever the validity of that claim, a good mirror, such as the Gerber (Portland, Oregon) is worth its weight (seven-tenths of an ounce) in self assurance alone. The Safe Signal (Tucson, Arizona) one-and-a-half ounces in its neoprene, floating, Velcro carrying case may be used conventionally, or in conjunction with a flashlight for night signaling.

- **Heat Packs:** Heat packs are now available for body, hands, and feet. Each pack will keep you warm for a couple of hours.

- **Plastic Garbage Bags:** Along with duct tape, the large plastic garbage bag has become the most popular take-along item for snow outings. Waterproof emergency clothes, ground sheet, pack cover, tarp, waterproof stuff-bag—you name it, the plastic bag can do it. Trash compactor bags, slightly smaller than conventional garbage bags, are three times stronger.

- **Whistle:** A whistle screech carries further than human voices.

- **Cellular Phone:** Now a standard unit for emergency purposes only.
- **Wristwatch:** Rugged, superior time-keeping watches may be purchased for less than $15.00.

Winter First Aid Kits
by Amy Matl

"Danger, the mountains and trees do not care! Be prepared for extreme changes in weather conditions." Signs at the entrances to our National Parks deliver an important message to visitors. It is a message that should be taken seriously by any adventurer entering a wilderness setting.

When preparing for a backcountry trip, you would-n't consider leaving without a sleeping bag and stove designed for the conditions you anticipate encounter-ing. Neither should you consider setting forth without the proper first aid kit. Just as the right sleeping bag can prevent disasters from occurring, the proper first aid kit can save your life. Consider too the persons you choose to venture into the great outdoors with. Those most likely to benefit from your preparedness are the people that are nearest and dearest to you. Most folks are found skiing, snowshoeing, or camping with close friends and family members.

So you decide to look into the first aid kits at your local outdoor store. Just as you might find the differ-ences in sleeping bag features confusing, so too might the different first aid kits make your head spin. Gener-ally, a commercially manufactured first aid kit will have been designed by medical experts. Folks that make their living working with medicine in backcountry set-tings are likely to include items you might overlook. This comprehensive selection of materials, coupled with the manufacturer's eye for organization, will make a commercial kit easier to use than a "homemade" kit packed in a Zip-Lock® bag.

As there are many outdoor activities, so too are there many activity-specific first aid kits. Bikers, hikers, campers, and skiers should choose the kit designed to meet their specific needs. The one you buy should address your answers to the following questions: How many people will be in your party? Where will you be traveling? Over what kind of terrain? What kind of environmental conditions are possible? How far from the nearest medical facility will you be? Do you or your companions have any medical training? And what level? Your answers will help determine the size and comprehensiveness of your first aid kit.

As a winter adventurer, your needs may go beyond the items included in a stock kit. In addition to wound cleaning components, sterile dressings, wound closure strips, medications, and latex gloves, your kit should include contents that address winter-specific injuries. Consider adding a tube of glucose for prevention of hypothermia—prevention is the best cure. For cold injuries such as frostbite, the same principle holds true. A couple of instant heat packs can stop an uncomfortable situation from becoming a disaster. A roll of cloth athletic tape is the best support for a sprained ankle. After strenuous exercise, like breaking trail through deep powder, a packet of electrolytes and a lot of water can quickly replenish what the body lost through sweating. Remember to attach a safety whistle to your kit. Should you be lost or injured you can use it to call for help. It will keep going after your voice has given out. There are many additional items that might be suggested, but then the kitchen sink could come in handy as well. Improvisation taught in wilderness specific first aid classes should cover any additional needs.

Now that you have a kit that is well suited for your activities, you need to insure that you know how to use it properly. First, familiarize yourself with the kit contents and where they are stored. Make note of any expiration dated contents. Medications, ointments, and topicals should have an expiration date. Although they probably won't be dangerous to use after their expiration dates have passed, they will become less effective. Check these dates each time before you leave for a trip.

The most important item in your kit, the instructions, should be given a lot of time and attention. Make sure you read them completely and carefully. A quality kit will contain an instruction sheet or book written by a wilderness medicine expert. It will be a comprehensive, concise, and easy-to-read road map of what is in your kit and how these contents should be used. Also covered will be basic first aid techniques used in treating common outdoor injuries. Reading these instructions carefully, before you put your kit away, will help to reduce the stress faced in a real life emergency. Remember: the kit is only as good as the user's training.

As a responsible participant in winter backcountry sports, it should be a priority to receive CPR and first aid training. If wilderness-specific courses are available in your area, they are highly recommended. As a backcountry adventurer, you are unable to carry all of the items found on an ambulance. A wilderness course teaches you to use the items found in your pack, and in nature around you, to deal with injuries that you encounter. The following organizations offer training in first aid and wilderness medicine:

WILDERNESS MEDICINE INSTITUTE
P.O. Box 9, 300 10th Street, Pitkin CO 81241, (970) 641-3572

SOLO

RFD 1 Box 163, Conway NH 03818, (603) 447-6711

WILDERNESS MEDICAL ASSOCIATES

RFD2, Box 890, Bryant Pond ME 04219, (207) 665-2707

WILDERNESS MEDICINE OUTFITTERS

2477 County Road 132, Elizabeth CO 80107, (303) 688-5176

The basic skills taught to students before entering a winter backcountry situation will help to minimize the potential need for first aid. Coupled with wilderness first aid training and common sense, a commercial kit should treat almost any injury you might encounter on a winter adventure. "Danger—the mountains and trees do not care!" Be prepared!

Global Positioning Units and Telephones

A relatively new high-tech tool called a Global Positioning System unit has entered the outdoor recreation market. The hand held unit, currently about the size of a cordless telephone, receives a radio signal from three (or four) orbiting satellites, 12,000 to 13,000 miles up, whose positions are known to a high degree of accuracy. The time elapsed between the transmission and receipt of the signal is translated into miles by the GPS unit and thus a "line" from the satellite to the unit. The intersection of three such mileage "lines" pinpoint only two possible sites, one of which may be wholly unreasonable and may be discarded. (A fourth reading eliminates the false second site.) The system was developed by the U.S. Department of Defense as a planet-wide navigation system. Upon completion, the 12 billion dollar project will encompass a constellation of 24 GPS satellites.

Currently, the less expensive GPS units operate to an accuracy of 60 to 100 feet, but proponents are talking of future low priced units with accuracy to be measured in inches. They also state that, in time, GPS will supersede dozens of the tools now in use to find our way, not only across the wilderness, but in rural areas and on city streets as well. For the present, GPS is certainly a major safety tool for backwoods travel, particularly in uncharted areas and cross-country ventures. Good GPS units have sold for less than $180 in 1996.

Whether many hikers will object to GPS units as instruments destructive of the wilderness experience is a question, but cellular telephones have already created controversy. Certainly, almost all hikers would object to casual use of a phone on a mountaintop rest break to inquire about mundane home affairs. Such workday disturbances are precisely what backcountry trekkers hope to escape. However, cellular phones have already saved lives and will save even more in the future. Certainly, any parent would argue that a boy or girl scout leader would be negligent in leading a troop of youngsters into the wilderness without a phone. The arguments against phones appear to be dwindling and will probably expire for all but a few diehards (there are still individuals who argue that a compass or a multi-purpose tool ruins the true backwoods experience) if the phone is carried deep inside the pack and is never to be seen except in an emergency.

Exercise—Warm Up, Cool Down

All outdoor recreationists should warm up before an outing and cool down afterwards, but such a regimen is particularly important in the cold season. If you have a recommended set of stretch and warm-up exercises for your particular sport, apply them before and after your trip. *(See guidelines on next page.)*

PREPARATIONS
Warm Up & Cool Down

It is very important that you "warm up" prior to your outdoor excursion, and "cool down" at the end. The following exercises will stretch the muscles used in walking and will reduce the possibility of injury and muscle soreness. The same stretches are used for warm up and cool down.

Stand with your feet about shoulder width apart, and toes pointed straight ahead. Keeping your knees slightly bent (1 inch), place one hand on your hip for support while you extend your other arm up and over your head. Now, slowly bend at your waist to the side, toward the hand on your hip. Move slowly; feel a good stretch. Hold and relax. Hold the stretch for 10-15 seconds. Always come out of a stretch slowly and under control. No quick or jerky movements.

Using a tree for balance, pull your knee toward your chest. Do not lean forward at the waist or hips. This gently stretches your upper hamstrings, butt and hips. The foot on the ground should be pointed straight ahead, with the knee slightly bent (1 inch). Hold the stretch for 15 seconds. Alternate legs.

To stretch your calf, stand a little ways from a tree, and lean on it with your forearms, head resting on hands. Bend one leg and place your foot on the ground in front of you, with the other leg straight behind. Slowly move your hips forward, keeping your lower back flat. Be sure to keep the heel of the straight leg on the ground, with toes pointed straight ahead or slightly turned in as you hold the stretch. Hold an easy stretch for 15 seconds. Do not bounce. Alternate legs.

To stretch the thigh and knee, hold the top of your right foot with your left hand, and gently pull your heel toward your buttocks. The knee bends at a natural angle when you hold your foot with the opposite hand. Hold for 15 seconds. Alternate legs.

Food

Eat before you start your snowshoe or Nordic ski trip, and sip water and nibble frequently during the outing. Eat before you get hungry; drink before you get thirsty. The Tahoe Nordic Search and Rescue Team recommends that you eat continually during your outing to replace expended energy. Your snacks and lunch should include a small amount of sugar foods such as jelly and some candy for quick energy (simple carbohydrates), a large selection of bread, bagels, crackers, pasta, fruit, vegetables, and cereals for long-term energy (complex carbohydrates), some meat or fish, beans, nuts, tofu for body maintenance (protein), and cheese, salami, nuts, peanut butter, chocolate to help you keep active and warm at night (fats).

Carbohydrates are the main fuel for the body and in normal circumstances should provide up to 70% of your calorie intake. On winter outings the percentage may drop as low as 55% to allow for a greater percentage of protein and fat.

Proteins are the material required for body maintenance, tissue repair and growth. Proteins come primarily from animal products such as meat, fish, poultry, cheese and eggs. However, protein is also available in cereal grains, beans, peas, and tofu. Outdoor winter sports require between 15% to 20% protein calories daily.

Fats provide twice the energy source of carbohydrates or proteins, but they carry triple the caloric intake on a weight-for-weight basis. Nonetheless, fats, which should make up less than 30% of the general public's daily caloric intake (many authorities are now leaning to less than 25%), may go as high as 40% for winter sports enthusiasts on the trail, particularly snow campers (summer intake should remain at 25%, though many outdoor people thrive on 15% fat calories daily).

Winter hiking or camping provides a unique food opportunity—you may "pig out" on high calorie foods with no sense of guilt. A man who might burn 2500 calories on a summer trek may find that the same hike in winter may require 4000 calories. Some authorities recommend hot chocolate and sugar in hot cereal in addition to your regular breakfast. Bread, sausage, cheese, nuts, and Snickers candy bars are good for lunch, and soups enriched with margarine and good portions of meat, fish, or cheese for dinner.

To summarize:

	Carbohydrates	Proteins	Fats
General Public	55-65%	15-20%	20-30%
Summer Backpackers	60-70%	15-20%	15-25%
Winter Campers	45-50%	15-20%	30-40%

Unbalanced nutrition will not occur on a one-day outing (and is very unlikely on a five- or six-day back-pack), but, nonetheless, nutritionists recommend food intake, in moderation, across the food spectrum. Eat from every food group and eat frequently. While on the trail on foot, snowshoe, or skis it is advisable to graze constantly. Carry an easy to reach belly pouch and nibble on bagels, crackers, dried fruit, granola, trail mix, sports bars, and an occasional chocolate candy bar. (Similarly, your water bottle should be easily accessible and you should sip as you graze.) On winter outings eat more than your usual workaday regimen. Leave your diet at home. Backcountry travel requires sustenance, particularly in the cold weather. On winter outings you should consume 3000 to 4500 calories daily (large men up to 5000 and small women about 2700 calories), and all food intake should be accompanied by lots and lots of water.

Drink plentifully throughout the day (no alcoholic beverages). Do not eat snow. Melting snow in your mouth saps energy and cools your body core.

Water

Snowshoers and Nordic skiers should carry water supplies sufficient for the full day, since it is unlikely that the smaller streams will be flowing or accessible under the snow. Water bottles should be available immediately (day-pack removal should be unnecessary) so that the 'shoer or skier may sip easily and often.

However, even winter sports people, particularly snow campers, should be aware of the risks associated with backcountry water. While there may be pockets of clean water in the wilderness, backcountry medical professionals recommend that water contamination should be regarded as the norm in the woods. All water should be treated to eliminate waterborne pathogens.

Boiling

For snow campers, bringing fresh, clean snow to a melt is sufficient to assure potability. Be sure to avoid watermelon snow (sometimes called red or pink snow) which is a sure sign of the algae Chlamydamonos Nivalis, which produces a toxin, Sorbitol, and may lead to severe stomach distress. Dr. Eric Weiss, Associate Director of Trauma and Emergency Medicine at the Stanford Medical Center also cautions against snow that may have been subject to flushing from high watercourses and thus possibly contaminated. Bringing snowmelt (or any water) to a boil is one of the most frequently used and most effective purification methods, but boiling time recommendations vary from heating water to 158°F for three minutes, to a rolling boil for one minute at sea level (5 minutes at 10,000 feet for the boiling point drops as the altitude increases), to a rolling boil for 20 minutes. However, Dr. Weiss says that just bringing water to a boil renders it safe to drink and that altitude does not require additional boiling time.

Filtration

Since a large volume of snow reduces to a small amount of water, the boiling process is tedious and time consuming, and requires a considerable measure of fuel. Thus, if a water source is available, mechanical filtration is often used to remove the three types of microorganisms that infect waters: 1) protozoa such as giardia and cryptosporidium, tough body, cystic parasites able to resist heat, freezing, iodine, and chlorine, and can exist for months; 2) bacteria such as salmonella, E. coli, and cholera, frail organisms with short life cycles, many less than one day; and, 3) viruses like hepatitis and Norwalk virus which have not occasioned a serious epidemic outbreak in North America in the last 50 years. Some chemicals like asbestos and dioxin may also be found in American waters.

Protozoa: Protozoa infest waters throughout North America and may be spread by humans and animals. Since the protective shells of protozoan cysts are resistant to iodine, filtration must serve to remove them.

Bacteria: Bacteria are also spread by humans and animals and, though not as prevalent as protozoa, are nonetheless a potential threat to all backcountry recreationists. Most bacteria can be removed by filtration, but several types are small enough to pass through a filter. This latter group may be rendered ineffective with a supplementary iodine disinfectant.

Viruses: Viruses spread by human contact are not a threat in North American water sources. However, many filters now add an iodine cartridge to the ceramic wafer to kill or remove all pathogens.

Filtration forces water by pump action, through a ceramic filter with pores small enough to trap the microorganisms. (Ceramic pores are generally 0.4 microns across though some authorities insist on 0.2

microns.) These one step filters are sometimes designated as "device" instruments. A "purifier," on the other
hand, uses an iodinated cartridge in conjunction with
the filter to effect disinfection.

Chemical Treatment

Some snow campers resort to the chemical treatment of water, attracted by the convenience of simple,
commercially-available products, and to protect against
possible filter freeze-up.

Iodine Tablets

Iodine tablets (TGHP-tetraglycine hydroperiodide)
come under the trade names of Potable-Aqua, Globa-
line, and Coughlans. The pre-measured dosage (8ppm)
requires one tablet to one quart of cool to warm water
(40-60°F, 15-20°C) or two tablets in cold or cloudy water. Let the mix stand for one hour in cold water before
use. The resulting taste may be masked with the addition of lemonade (or other) crystals. The citrus crystals
should be added after the contact period. The iodine
tablets are unstable when exposed to air and should be
discarded about three or four months after first opening
the bottle.

Tincture of Iodine (2 percent)

Six to eight drops (10 drops if the water is cold or
cloudy) per quart is effective. Let the treated water
stand for one hour before use. Citrus drink crystals
may be added after the contact period.

Iodine Crystals

Iodine crystals are a bit too picky for anyone with a
high impatience factor, but on long treks, some snowshoers find them best. Fill a one-ounce (liquid) brown
bottle with water and six grams of iodine crystals (from
your local pharmacy or chemical supply house). Shake

the bottle vigorously and let the crystals settle. Pour half the liquid (about 1 tablespoon) into your quart water bottle (be certain no crystals drop into your canteen). Wait one hour before use. Refill your one ounce bottle with clear water. It may be refilled time and again until all the iodine crystals have dissolved.

For snow trekkers who want to use the iodine crystal method but wish to avoid the fuss, Polar-pure makes a kit, available from most outdoor stores, complete with pre-measured crystals and an amber bottle which weighs three ounces.

Chlorine, Halazone Tablets

These tablets release chlorine (1 tablet per quart) into your drinking water. Chlorine is fairly effective against some pathogens, but not against giardia. Wait 20 minutes before use. Halazone deteriorates rapidly. Take a fresh bottle on each long trip.

Liquid Bleach

Liquid bleach, with 4 to 6 percent available chlorine, may be used for water purification. Two drops of bleach in a quart of water (4 drops in cold or murky water) is the standard. Let the treated water stand one hour before use. Bleach is also useful for cleanup, particularly camping wash-up. Use a spoonful of bleach in the final rinse water to sterilize dishes and flatware.

For hikers who find chemical water treatment doses listed only in cc's, figure about 15cc to one tablespoon; in milliliters one drop equals .05 milliliters. Since chemical treatment recommendations now suggest a one-hour wait before use, it is advisable to carry two canteens, one for immediate use and the second as your "treatment" bottle—alternating between them, of course.

Winter Hazards

Avalanches

There are several types of avalanches—snow, ice, rock, and mud. Throughout this section, we shall discuss snow avalanches exclusively, and the information presented is derived from a variety of U.S. Forest Service publications. Snow avalanches, even small avalanches, can hold mammoth power and represent a serious threat to winter sports enthusiasts. Naturally, the more time one spends in snow backcountry, the greater are the chances of being caught in an avalanche. To avoid possible capture by a snowslide, one should know the types of avalanches, terrain, and weather conditions which contribute to such disasters, and the safest terrain in crossing avalanche territory. Such knowledge will assist the winter recreationist to steer clear of snow slides, and even to survive if buried by such a snow torrent.

The two basic types of avalanches are "loose snow" and "slab." Loose snow avalanches start at a small area or a single point. The snow volume increases as does the area covered as the loose snow descends, forming an inverted V. There is little internal cohesion in a loose snowslide, and the snow plunges as a formless mass.

Slab avalanches, on the other hand, start when a large area of snow begins to slide all at once. There is a well-defined fracture line where the moving snow breaks away from the stable snow. Slab avalanches are characterized by the tendency of snow crystals to stick together. There may be angular blocks or chunks of snow in the slide. Practically all accidents are caused by slab avalanches. Many times, the victims have triggered the avalanche themselves. Their weight on the stressed snow slab is enough to break the fragile bonds that hold it to the slope.

Terrain Factors

There are four terrain factors affecting snow avalanches: slope steepness, slope profile, slope aspect, and ground cover.

Slope steepness. Avalanches are most common on slopes of 30 to 45 degrees (60 to 100 percent), but large avalanches can occur on slopes ranging from 25 to 60 degrees. The diagram below shows the slopes where avalanches are most common.

Slope profile. Dangerous slab avalanches are more likely to occur on convex slopes, but may also occur on concave slopes. Short slopes may be as dangerous as long slopes!

Slope aspect. Snow on north-facing slopes is more likely to slide in midwinter. South-facing slopes are dangerous in the spring and on sunny days. Leeward slopes are dangerous because wind-deposited snows add depth and create hard, hollow-sounding wind slabs. Windward slopes, generally, have less snow, the snow is compacted, and usually strong enough to resist movement.

Ground cover. Large rocks, trees, and heavy brush help anchor the snow, but avalanches can start even among trees. Smooth, grassy slopes are more dangerous.

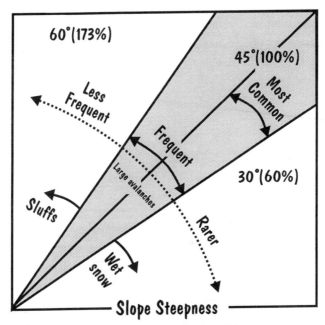

60°(173%)

45°(100%)

Most Common

Less Frequent

Frequent

Large avalanches

30°(60%)

Sluffs

Rarer

Wet snow

Slope Steepness

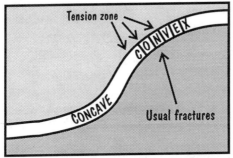

Tension zone

CONVEX

CONCAVE

Usual fractures

Snow is anchored

Snow slides easily

Rule of Thumb: If, on skis, you can move through a wooded area, so can an avalanche.

Weather Factors

Many weather factors affect the chances of a snow avalanche occurring: temperature, wind, storms, rate of snowfall, and types of snow.

Temperature. Snow persists in an unstable condition under cold temperatures. It will settle and stabilize rapidly when temperatures are near, or just above, freezing. Storms starting with low temperatures and dry snow, followed by rising temperatures, are more likely to cause avalanches. The dry snow at the start forms a poor bond and has insufficient strength to support the heavier snow deposited late in the storm. Rapid changes in weather conditions (wind, temperature, snowfall) cause snowpack adjustments. Such adjustments may affect snowpack stability and cause an avalanche. Therefore, be alert to weather changes.

Wind. Sustained winds of 15 miles per hour and over rapidly increase the danger of an avalanche occurring. Snow plumes from ridges and peaks indicate that snow is being moved onto leeward slopes. This can create dangerous conditions.

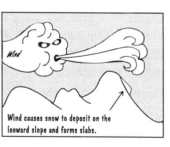
Wind causes snow to deposit on the leeward slope and forms slabs.

Storms. A high percentage (about 80 percent) of all avalanches occur during, and shortly after, storms. Be extra cautious during those periods. Loose, dry snow slides easily. Moist, dense snow tends to settle rapidly, but during windy periods can be dangerous.

Rate of snowfall. Snow falling at the rate of one inch per hour or more rapidly increases avalanche danger.

Crystal types. Snow-crystal types may be examined by letting them fall on a dark ski mitt or parka sleeve. Small crystals—needles and pellets—result in more dangerous conditions than the usual star-shaped crystals.

For weather information, check the local weather forecasts. Contact the Forest Service snow ranger or the nearest winter sports area ski patrol.

General Observations

Look for signs of recent avalanche activity and old slide paths; listen for sounds and cracks; be alert to snow conditions.

Recent avalanche activity. If you see new avalanche evidence, suspect dangerous conditions. Beware when snowballs or "cartwheels" roll down the slope.

Old slide paths. Generally, avalanches occur in the same areas. Watch for avalanche paths. Look for pushed-over small trees, trees with limbs broken off. Avoid steep, open gullies, and slopes.

Sounds and cracks. If the snow sounds hollow, particularly on a leeward slope, conditions are probably dangerous. If the snow cracks and the cracks continue to form, this indicates slab avalanche danger is high.

New snow. Be alert to dangerous conditions with one foot or more of new snow.

Old snow. When the old snow depth is sufficient to cover natural anchors—such as rocks and brush—additional snow layers will slide more readily. The nature of the old snow surface is important. Rough surfaces favor stability; smooth surfaces, such as sun crusts, are less stable. A loose, underlying snow layer is more dangerous than a compacted one. Check the underlying snow layer with a ski pole, ski, or rod.

Wet snow. Rainstorms or spring weather with warm winds and cloudy nights can warm the snow

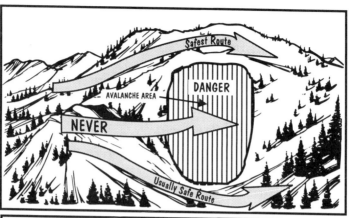

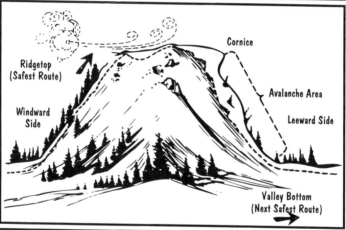

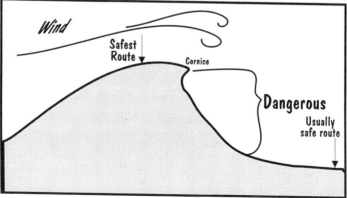

cover. The resulting free and percolating water may cause wet snow avalanches. Wet snow avalanches are more likely on south slopes and slopes under exposed rock.

Route Selection and Precautions

The safest routes are on ridgetops and slightly on the windward side, away from cornices. Windward slopes are usually safer than leeward slopes. If you cannot travel on the ridges, the next safest route is out in the valley, far from the bottom of slopes. Avoid disturbing cornices from below or above. Gain ridgetops by detouring around cornice areas. If you must cross dangerous slopes, stay high and near the top. If you see avalanche fracture lines in the snow, avoid them and similar snow areas. If you must ascend or descend a dangerous slope, go straight up or down; do not make traverses back and forth across the slope. Take advantage of areas of dense timber, ridges, or rocky outcrops as islands of safety. Use them for lunch and rest stops. Spend as little time as possible on open slopes.

Obey signs closing slopes due to avalanche danger. Only one person at a time should cross a dangerous slope. All others should watch him. Remove ski pole straps and ski safety straps, loosen all equipment, put on mittens and cap, and fasten clothing before you travel in any areas where there is avalanche danger. Carry and use an avalanche cord; carry a sectional probe.

Avalanche Survival

If you are caught in an avalanche:
- Discard all equipment.
- Make swimming motions. Try to stay on top; work your way to the side of the avalanche.

- Before coming to a stop, get your hands in front of your face and try to make an air space in the snow as you are coming to a stop.
- Try to remain calm.

If you are the survivor:
- Mark the place where you last saw victims.
- Search for victims directly downslope below the last seen point. If they are not on the surface, probe the snow with a pole or stick.
- You are the victim's best hope for survival.
- Do not desert victims and go for help unless help is only a few minutes away. Remember, you must consider not only the time required to get help, but the time required for help to return. After 30 minutes, the buried victim has only a 50 percent chance of surviving.

If there is more than one survivor:
- Send one for help while the others search for the victim. Have the one who goes for help mark the route so a rescue party can follow back.
- Contact the ski patrol, local sheriff, or Forest Service.
- Administer first aid.
- Treat for suffocation and shock.

Avalanche Rescue Beacons

Avalanche beacons are small, lightweight personal radio transmitter/receivers (transceivers) which have been on the market since 1968 and saved scores of lives since that time. The transceivers are standard issue for all ski patrols, search and rescue squads and winter highway patrols, and are being recommended increasingly for groups of backcountry recreationists. At the start of a winter wilderness trek, every participant attaches a beacon firmly to his/her body and sets it to *transmit* (all avalanche beacons now operate at 457 Hz). When an avalanche overtakes the group, all survivors immediately switch their beacons to *receive*, and by employing a gridded search pattern (the beacons do not work on a straight directional basis), that is a series of ever narrowing right-angle turns, they can hone in on the snow-buried unit(s). Since speed is vital to the full recovery of the buried victims, beacons are the surest means for the rapid discovery of those individuals. The search process may be learned in half a day and a trained operator can locate a buried beacon in less than five minutes of the receipt of the first signal.

Avalanche Probes

Avalanche probes are lightweight metal (usually aluminum) folding rods about one-half inch across, which may be opened to form a compact, long slim pole (probe) about ten feet long. The probe is pressed carefully into avalanche debris at the suspected point of a buried victim to find a solid spot indicative of a body. Many ski or snowshoe poles are designed to release their baskets and snap together. Fully extended, these poles can act as probes.

Travel On Ice

Travel over frozen lakes, ponds, or streams may be hazardous. If you are the least bit uncertain, assume that the ice is unsafe. The Cold Region Research and Engineering Laboratory in Hanover, New Hampshire recommends the following basic rules. The pond or lake ice should be at least two inches thick to support one person on a ten-foot-square section, and four inches thick for two persons. When out with a group, watch for cracks. If possible, drill a hole in the ice and take note of the water level. If the water reaches the top of the ice and begins to spill over, all group members should slowly walk toward land. Do not run because running can create waves which fracture the ice. Most important: use common sense and do not go out alone.

Hypothermia

Be aware of the danger of hypothermia—subnormal temperature of the body. Lowering of internal temperature of the body leads to mental and physical collapse.

Hypothermia is caused by exposure to cold, and is aggravated by wet, wind, and exhaustion. It is the number one killer of outdoor recreationists.

Seven Steps To Hypothermia
How The Body Loses Heat

1. **Radiation**—Heat loss through the skin. The head is the greatest radiator. Wear a hat!

2. **Conduction**—Touching cold surfaces such as snow, ice, metals, and fuels. Wear gloves!

3. **Convection**—Wind moves warm air quickly from clothing and body. Wear windproof clothes and get out of the wind!

4. **Evaporation**—Fast, excessive sweat loss. Wear clothes that get perspiration off the skin. Avoid undue sweating by adjusting layers of clothes. Keep warm, but try not to sweat excessively.

5. **Respiration**—Inhaling cold air and exhaling warm air causes great internal heat loss. In severe weather, breathe in through a headband and out through the mouth.

6. **Wind Chill**—Accompanying wind magnifies the severity of cold temperatures. A breeze of only 2 miles per hour can greatly increase perceived cold. Wear windproof clothes and get out of the wind.

7. **Water Chill**—The thermal conductivity of water is 240 times that of still air! Wet clothing can extract heat 240 times faster than dry clothes! Water is considered one of nature's greatest conductors of heat. Change out of wet clothes as soon as possible.

Cold Kills in Two Distinct Steps: *The first step is exposure and exhaustion.* The moment you begin to lose heat faster than your body produces it, you are undergoing exposure. Two things happen: you voluntarily exercise to stay warm, and your body makes involuntary adjustments to preserve normal temperature in the vital organs. Both responses drain your energy reserves. The only way to stop the drain is to reduce the degree of exposure. The time to prevent hypothermia is during this period of exposure and gradual exhaustion.

The second step is hypothermia. If exposure continues until your energy reserves are exhausted, cold reaches the brain, depriving you of judgment and reasoning power. You will not be aware that this is happening. You will lose control of your hands. This is hypothermia. Your internal temperature is sliding downward. Without treatment, this slide leads to stupor, collapse, and death.

Symptoms: If your party is exposed to wind, cold, and wet, **think hypothermia**. Watch yourself and others for symptoms.
• Uncontrollable fits of shivering.
• Vague, slow, slurred speech.
• Memory lapses, incoherence.
• Immobile, fumbling hands.
• Frequent stumbling. Lurching gait.
• Drowsiness—to sleep is to die.
• Apparent exhaustion. Inability to get up after a rest.

Treatment: The victim may deny he is in trouble. Believe the symptoms, not the victim. Even mild symptoms demand immediate, drastic treatment.
• Get the victim out of the wind and rain.
• Strip off all wet clothes.
• If the victim is only mildly impaired, give him warm drinks. Get him into warm clothes and a warm

sleeping bag. Well-wrapped, warm (not hot) rocks or canteens will hasten recovery.

- If the victim is semi-conscious or worse, try to keep him awake. Give him warm drinks. Leave him stripped. Put the victim in a sleeping bag with another person— also stripped. If you have a double bag, put the victim between two warm donors. Skin to skin contact is the most effective treatment.
- Build a fire to warm the camp.

Prevention: Defense Against Hypothermia— Stay dry. When clothes get wet, they lose about 90 percent of their insulating value. Wool and some synthetics lose less; cotton and down lose more. Choose rain clothes that are proof against wind-driven rain and cover head, neck, body, and legs. Breathable waterproof garments are best. Polyurethane coated nylon will keep the rain out, but it will keep the perspiration in, and the coatings won't last forever. Inspect coated nylon garments carefully and test under a cold shower before you leave home. Ponchos are poor protection from the wind.

Beware of the wind. A slight breeze carries heat away from bare skin much faster than still air. Wind drives cold air under and through clothing. Wind refrigerates wet clothes by evaporating moisture from the surface. Wind multiplies the problem of staying dry. Take synthetic fleece or woolen clothing for hypothermia weather. Wear two-piece synthetic underwear, long wool pants and a sweater or shirt. Include a hat or balaclava that can protect neck and chin. Cotton underwear is worse than useless when wet; cotton kills!

Understand cold. Most hypothermia cases develop in air temperatures between 30 and 50 degrees. Most outdoorsmen can't believe such temperatures can be dangerous. They underestimate the danger of being wet at such temperatures—with fatal results. Fifty-degree water is unbearably cold. The cold that kills is cold water running down neck and legs and cold water held against the body by wet clothes, flushing heat from the body.

Use your clothes. Put on raingear before you get wet. Put on warm clothes before you start shivering.

End exposure. If you cannot stay dry and warm under existing weather conditions, using the clothes you have with you, end your exposure to the elements immediately. Be smart enough to forego reaching the peak or making that last run or whatever else may entice you to stay out when wet or cold.

Get out of the wind and rain. Build a fire. Concentrate on making your camp or bivouac as secure and comfortable as possible. Never ignore shivering. Persistent or violent shivering is clear warning that you are on the verge of hypothermia. A stormproof tent gives best shelter. Take plastic sheeting and nylon twine with you for rigging additional foul-weather shelter.

Carry trail food—nuts, jerky, candy—and keep nibbling during hypothermia weather. Take a camp stove or a long-burning candle, flammable paste, or other reliable firestarters. Don't wait for an emergency. Use these items to avoid or minimize exposure. Take heed of "hypothermia weather." Watch carefully for warning symptoms. Choose equipment with hypothermia in mind. **Think hypothermia.**

Forestall exhaustion. Make camp while you still have a reserve of energy and allow for the fact that exposure greatly reduces your normal endurance. Be aware that exercise drains energy reserves. If exhaustion forces you to stop, however briefly, your body heat production instantly drops 50 percent or more. Violent, incapacitating shivering may begin immediately, and you may slip into hypothermia in a matter of minutes.

Appoint a foul-weather leader. Make the best-protected member of your party responsible for calling a halt before the least-protected member becomes exhausted or goes into violent shivering.

Wind Chill

Wind, temperature, and moisture are factors which can greatly affect the safety of a winter traveler. Each contributes to the loss of body heat. The "wind chill" chart illustrates the effect of wind and temperatures on a dry, properly clothed person. If clothing is wet from perspiration or precipitation, the net effect of wind and temperature is much greater.

Wind Speed Cooling Power Expressed as "Equivalent Temperature"

mph	Temperature (F)											
Calm	40	30	20	10	5	0	-10	-20	-30	-40	-50	-60
	Equivalent Chill Temperature											
5	35	25	15	5	0	-5	-15	-25	-35	-45	-55	-70
10	30	15	5	-10	-15	-20	-35	-45	-60	-70	-80	-95
15	25	10	-5	-20	-25	-30	-45	-60	-70	-85	-100	-110
20	20	5	-10	-25	-30	-35	-50	-65	-80	-95	-110	-120
25	15	0	-15	-30	-35	-45	-60	-75	-90	-105	-120	-135
30	10	0	-20	-30	-40	-50	-65	-80	-95	-110	-125	-140
35	10	-5	-20	-35	-40	-50	-65	-80	-100	-115	-130	-145
40	10	-5	-20	-35	-45	-55	-70	-85	-100	-115	-130	-150
	Danger			Increasing Danger (Flesh may freeze within 1 minute)			Great Danger (Flesh may freeze within 30 seconds)					

Example: At a wind speed of 20 mph, an ambient temperature of 20 degrees Fahrenheit is equivalent to minus 10 degrees Fahrenheit.

Dehydration

An adult at rest requires 2 quarts of water daily. Up to 4 quarts are required for strenuous activity. There is a 25% loss of stamina when an adult loses 1 quart of water. Avoid dehydration—simply drink as often as you feel thirsty. Better yet, drink before you get thirsty.

Frostbite

Frostbite is caused by exposure of inadequately protected flesh to subfreezing temperatures. Tissue damage is caused by the reduced blood flow to the extremities, as opposed to hypothermia, which causes lowering of the body's rate of metabolism.

Symptoms:

Mild: Redness, inflammation, stinging.

Moderate: Skin gray or mottled white and soft to pressure, intense stinging.

Severe: Skin waxy white, hard or stiff, swollen, loss of sensation.

Treatment: Restore body temperature as rapidly as possible, preferably by immersion in a water bath of less than 110° temperature, by hot coffee or tea, or by any other means available. If necessary to continue the trek, the affected part should be kept dry and covered and the victim moved, as quickly as possible, to a location where effective treatment and/or vehicle evacuation can be obtained.

Most frequently, isolated parts of the body: cheeks, nose, hands, and feet are subject to frostbite. Gently cover ears and nose with warm hands. If feet are frostbitten, place cotton between the toes and try to keep the victim from placing weight on the foot. Never attempt to rewarm the affected area by rubbing or massaging, and do not allow the sufferer to smoke (nicotine constricts arteries and hinders blood flow). Bear in mind that the patient may experience severe pain as the affected part thaws and recovers.

Prevention: Party members should periodically observe their companions, especially nose and cheeks, for signs of frostbite. Snowmobilers, due to their speed of travel, are particularly susceptible to frostbite.

Altitude Sickness

At 10,000 feet, air contains only two-thirds of the volume of oxygen that it does at sea level. In addition, the higher air pressure at sea level easily forces the available oxygen through the thin lining of the lungs into the bloodstream. At higher elevations there is less air pressure and it is more difficult for the available oxygen to be forced through the lung walls.

Symptoms: Nausea, dizziness, fatigue, and drowsiness as well as weakness, apathy, listlessness and loss of appetite.

Treatment: Stop and rest, breathe deeply several times, obtain nourishment from simple sugar, like candy or fruit juices. Take aspirin or ibuprofen and travel as soon as possible to lower elevations. If possible, spend a night or two at an intermediate elevation between home and destination. A gradual increase in elevation will help the body acclimatize. Eat a high carbohydrate diet prior to and during the trip. Stoke up on pasta, rice, bread, and potatoes, and drink water frequently. Reduce or eliminate alcohol, tranquilizers, and sleeping pills from your regimen. Such substances may decrease your body's ability to adjust to higher elevations. Acclimate yourself with a day of light exercise at the higher elevation before a major trip, and try to limit your ascent to less than 2000 feet a day on your trip. Altitude sickness, or acute mountain sickness is not life threatening and sufferers will recover after a few uncomfortable days provided they follow the prescription to move to lower altitudes. (Note: Two other altitude-associated illnesses, pulmonary edema and cerebral edema, are almost always associated with extreme heights, over 14,000 feet, and can be life threatening.)

Prevention: Keep in good physical condition and eat a well-balanced diet. Avoid sudden trips which involve immediate physical exercise (climbing) to high altitudes.

Hyperventilation

Symptoms: This reaction to altitude is caused by too-rapid breathing and decrease of the carbon dioxide level in the blood, causing light-headedness and a sense of cold. Victims are apprehensive and excited.

Treatment: Calm the victim, have him relax and breathe into a glove, bag, or hat until normal breathing is restored.

Prevention: Same as for altitude sickness.

Lost or Injured Party

A good map, skill with a compass, and pre-planning will minimize the possibility of getting lost. Check weather forecasts and avoid storms. It is easy to become disoriented in the whiteouts of winter or when physically exhausted.

If you are lost, sustain an injury, are overcome by fatigue, break a ski, experience a snowmobile engine failure, or encounter any emergency situation, use the S.T.O.P. system:

S—Stop. Find a safe place nearby and stay put. The farther you go, the harder it may be to find you. Don't waste energy in aimless wandering.

T—Think. Evaluate your situation. Assess the condition of the individuals in your party. Can you resolve the problem? Should you backtrack for assistance or stay put and allow a search team to find you?

O—Observe. Check the area for any possible help for your predicament. Is there a sheltered area, a downed tree, a thicket out of the wind, a ledge for a snow cave, a space for a Quinzee?

P—Plan. Develop an action plan and implement it. Stay calm and optimistic. Working out a plan will allow you to avoid panic. Think positively and realize that your situation is temporary.

Stop as soon as you realize that you are lost. Keep calm. Evaluation of your situation will determine whether you backtrack, trusting your compass, or remain in place. If you decide to send for help, send at least two people. If you plan to remain, keep the party together and keep your spirits high with the knowledge that your situation is temporary.

Create a shelter, but build it *just* large enough to accommodate the party to conserve energy. If you have time and the knowledge, build a snow cave or a Quinzee. Otherwise, improvise with any materials at hand: snowshoes, skies, poles, large slabs of ice, tarps, ropes, garbage bags, anything that will help to keep you from wind, rain, or snow, and be particularly careful that it is not in avalanche territory. A tree out of the wind is always a good starting point. If possible, face the entrance east to catch the morning sun. Sit or lie on your mat or pack, stay off the snow. Create ground-to-air signals: stamp SOS in the snow, stamp a trail in four directions from your shelter or use the emergency ground-to-air signals code. Try to make yourself as visible as possible. If possible, light a fire and keep it going. Three of anything: three blasts of a whistle, three shouts, three flashes of light, three rocks, three packs, is a distress signal, a call for help.

Ground To Air Signals—Visible emergency signals are easily made in large open areas. SOS can be stamped in snowfields or grassy meadows. Brush piles or evergreen boughs can also be used. Listed below is the emergency code for ground to air signals.

I	**II**	**X**
Require doctor—serious injury	Require medical supplies	Unable to proceed
F	**V**	**↑**
Require food and water	Require assistance	Proceeding in this direction
Y	**N**	**LL**
Yes—affirmative	No—negative	All well

Overdue Party

When Someone Is Overdue—*Keep calm.* Notify the County Sheriff or District Ranger in the trip area. Either of these officers will take steps to alert or activate local search and rescue organization. If the missing person returns later, be sure to advise the Sheriff or Ranger.

Backcountry Safety

• Never travel alone.
• Select a travel route familiar to at least one member of your party and equal to your experience and ability.
• Consult a ranger station for the weather forecast, snow and avalanche conditions, touring routes, and equipment recommendations before departing.
• Postpone or terminate your trip if a storm is forecast or appears to be building.
• If caught in a storm, wait it out in a sheltered, avalanche-safe area until conditions stabilize.
• Be prepared for winter weather extremes (gale winds, subzero temperatures, blowing snow, whiteout conditions) which can kill the unprepared.

- Allow extra travel time during soft snow conditions.
- Keep a written note of the nearest ranger station or emergency telephone number for use in emergencies.
- Remember, you depend on your own good sense and resources for survival.

Snowshoe and Nordic Ski Safety Rules

- Nordic skiers should take lessons from a qualified instructor.
- Never take a solo winter trek. A group of three or four is optimum. In the event of an emergency injury, one or two companions can go for help while one stays with the patient.
- Never ski or 'shoe on a trail that is rated above your ability. Injury or equipment damage is frequently the result of an attempt at too difficult a climb or descent. Your trail should not be a trial.
- On trails shared with snowmobiles, be constantly alert for approaching vehicles, particularly those from the rear. Be especially wary on hills or curves which may conceal oncoming snowmobiles.
- Be sure to wear sunglasses and a brimmed hat, particularly on sunny days, and apply sunblock and lip pomade.
- Obey all route signs, particularly "closed area" notices.
- Carry extra clothes, and high energy food items.
- Snowshoers should never walk on a ski track, whether groomed or man-made.
- Give way to the downhill skier (or snowshoer); they have the right of way. When approaching other trekkers on the downhill trail shout, "track" to let them know you are coming. Yell it soon enough to allow those trekkers time to step out of the trail.

- If you stop for any reason (wax skis, put on skins) step off the trail but remain visible to oncoming skiers.
- Fill in all "sitzmarks" and any other snow holes you may make. Leave a consistent surface for other recreationists.
- Do not litter. Carry a zipper-locking plastic bag for your trash.
- Snowshoers should follow these good "hiking" recommendations:
  - Stretch before your outing.
  - Keep your breathing at a natural pace with your heart rate.
  - Always maintain good posture, with your lower back flat and pelvis tucked directly under your spine.
  - If you plan to 'shoe at a pace beyond strolling, it's important for your body temperature to rise gradually. So warm up for at least 5 to 10 minutes before increasing your speed.
  - Stretch *after* your outing, when your muscles are warm and more flexible.
  - 'Shoeing with ski poles helps you reach your target heart rate at a slower walking speed.
  - Relax. Control, rather than tense your muscles.
  - Take easy steps, not long strides. Try for the most natural stride.
  - To determine your target heart rate: walk fast enough to notice your breathing, but not so fast that you are out of breath or gasping. If conversing, you should have to pause regularly to breathe, but you should be able to talk.

Trail Symbols

Certain symbols may be posted at trailheads. Called "difficulty symbols," they classify the trail according to the ability of the skiers. Common trail markers also include a trailhead sign, trailblazer, and directional marker.

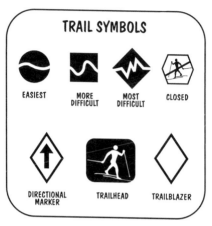

Alpine Ski Safety Rules

- Before your first run, familiarize yourself with the layout of the ski area. Decide which trails are within your ability level and note their locations.
- Take lessons from a qualified instructor. Learning to ski correctly will prevent the development of bad habits which may be difficult to break.
- Never ski alone. Keep your companions informed of your intentions.
- Stay within the ski area boundaries and obey all ski signs. Every lost skier and several deaths in the last decade have resulted from skiers deliberately or accidentally running outside the boundaries.
- Make sure your bindings are adjusted correctly and repeat that examination each time you remount your skis. Skis should be adjusted to separate from the boot in a moderate fall.
- Use mounted ski brakes or retention straps on your skis. Most ski resorts will not allow skiers on the slopes without some type of safety device to prevent runaway skis.

- If you sight a runaway ski, loudly shout "ski" in the direction the ski is heading to alert other skiers. A runaway ski can be extremely dangerous.
- Call it a day when your body says it is time for a rest. Skip that last run, which may turn out to be your very last run.

The Skier's Responsibility Code

Skiing can be enjoyed in many ways. At ski areas you may see people using alpine, snowboard, telemark, cross-country or other specialized ski equipment, such as that used by disabled or other skiers. Regardless of how you decide to enjoy the slopes, always show courtesy to others and be aware that there are elements of risk in skiing that common sense and personal awareness can help reduce. Observe the code listed below and share with other skiers the responsibility for a great skiing experience.

1. Always stay in control, and be able to stop or avoid other people or objects.
2. People ahead of you have the right of way. It is your responsibility to avoid them.
3. You must not stop where you obstruct a trail, or are not visible from above.
4. Whenever starting downhill or merging into a trail, look uphill and yield to others.
5. Always use devices to prevent runaway equipment.
6. Observe all posted signs and warnings. Keep off closed trails and out of closed areas.
7. Prior to using any lift, you must have the knowledge and ability to load, ride and unload safely.

Know The Code. It's Your Responsibility.

Additional Safety Precautions

1. Wear sunglasses and sunblock cream.
2. Don't ski blindly into unfamiliar areas. There are

ditches, drop offs, rocks, stumps, snowmaking equipment with guns possibly operating at various places on the side of the runs. Be especially cautious during foggy, snowy, or cloudy days. Dress warmly, as weather may change dramatically from the bottom of the mountain to the top.

3. Watch out for icy and slippery walks.

4. Be alert at the chairlift unloading stations. Be ready to get off, don't ride past the unloading point and if you do, DON'T jump out of the chair. The attendant will help you. If you fall while sliding down the ramp, move out of the way so you are not bumped by the next skier.

5. Never jump out of a chairlift at any point or at any time. Always use a designated unloading station.

6. Don't bounce or swing the chairlift chairs while riding.

7. If you see an accident, tell a Ski Patrolman or the nearest lift attendant.

Snowboard Safety Rules

Before your first run, familiarize yourself with the layout of the snowboard area. Decide on the trails that are within your ability level and note their locations.

• Never snowboard alone! The single most serious, and often fatal, accident for snowboarders is deep snow suffocation. Snowboarders who fall head first into a snow hole or upside-down in a drift cannot release their bindings to free themselves, and, thus, strangle. In 1994, at least 12 snowboard deaths occurred, most from suffocation, and 1995's death toll seems to be even higher. Boarders caught head down in deep snow can smother in a matter of minutes, so it is critical that they be freed from the snow immediately. Snowboarders who find themselves entrapped should try to create as large as possible an air pocket about their faces. Always run with companions; even non-fatal injuries require a partner to report the accident.

- Do not attempt to exceed your skill level. Choose trails within your ability. Secondary causes of snowboard death and injury are collisions with trees and rocks. Stay on terrain which will allows you to control your run.
- Keep your equipment in top condition.
- Do not go out in deep powder unless you are a top flight 'boarder, and even then, only with equally competent mates.
- Wait out whiteout conditions—stay in the lodge until you can see the slopes clearly. Similarly, call it a day when darkness prevents a full view of the area or when evening shadows may conceal pitfalls.
- Call it a day when your body says it is time for a break. Skip that last run.
- Avoid icy slopes which are impossible to control.
- Be especially wary around tree wells. These deep depressions are death traps waiting for the unwary.
- Stay within area bounds and obey all ski signs.
- Risk-taking has its bounds. Err on the side of safety.

Sledding Safety Rules

Sledding, which is associated in our memory with the most innocent and childish of winter pleasures, is actually one of the more dangerous winter sports. Many hospitals in winter sport areas report that sled injuries account for half the year's accidents. The Tahoe Forest Hospital notes that about 30 people per winter day are brought to the emergency room with snow-related injuries, and that sledding accounts for the most frequently cited cause and for many of the most serious injuries, such as spine fractures and serious head and neck trauma.

Three factors are primarily responsible for such a gross injury toll: the number and ages of sledding participants, the lack of any protective clothing or gear, and unsafe terrain. The director of emergency services at Tahoe Forest Hospital remarked that while it "may seem humorous...if one wants to protect a kid [when sledding] they should dress them like a motorcross bike rider."

Sleds may reach a speed of 20 miles per hour on a downhill run, and hitting a tree or another sledder, or flying off a bump at such a speed may result in serious injury. Basically, sleds (or saucers, inner tubes, plastic bags, cardboard sheets, and toboggans) are unsteerable, and trying to steer or stop with an outstretched leg can result in broken shins and mangled knees. Steep slopes and icy hills are other factors leading to harm.

- Inspect the sledding hill for potential hazards such as rocks, holes, and bumps.
- Wear protective clothing and headgear. A bicycle helmet over a winter hat is a good choice.
- Sit up in a sled, facing forward. Do not slide downhill head first in a prone position.
- Choose uncrowded slopes, free of trees and a reasonable grade for the sledder involved. Tots are generally happy with short easy runs (and a short walk back up the hill).
- Reject icy or hard-packed hills or any hill that dead ends at a road, a parking lot, or a lake or watercourse.
- Choose a snow-covered slope with a flat runout.

Snowmobile Safety

Practically all snowmobile manufacturers in North America meet the minimum safety standards set by the Snowmobile Safety and Certification Committee of the industry. The certificate is awarded after tests of the various machine systems: electric, lighting, brake, fuel and starting. The tests also include the controls: emergency brake and throttle, and the reflectors, handgrips, seats, shields, and guards. The awarded label is normally affixed in the right tunnel of the 'mobile. Be sure your machine shows that label.

At the start of each winter season, your machine should be treated to a full tune-up covering ignition, carburetor, lubrication, and the drive belt. Each of these items should be adjusted or replaced as necessary. In addition, the machine should be thoroughly checked in accordance with the operator's manual. Make all the required adjustments and be sure to follow the company's suggested safety recommendations. The pre-season check should be followed by a pre-start check before every outing: steering, throttle, brakes, lights, fuel. Before departure, leave word at home of the destined route and times of departure and return. If possible, leave the same information at the appropriate ranger station, where you may also inquire about backcountry snow and avalanche conditions.

Never travel alone. Always drive with friends so that emergency situations may be dealt with.

Learn to read snow and terrain conditions and drive accordingly. Iced-over slopes can be particularly difficult to traverse. Avoid crossing lakes and streams unless you are absolutely certain that the ice can carry your weight. If you must travel on waterways, check for safety and be sure to wear a personal flotation device. Night driving can also be hazardous. Slow down so as to stay within the safety range of your headlights, and avoid unfamiliar territory.

Snowmobiling is hazardous, and a safety course for beginners is a wise precaution. Snowmobilers require specialized clothing and added protection.

Clothing

The layering system described earlier is also recommended for snowmobilers except that the final "shell" layer may be a heavier special snowmobile suit. Such suits may be lined with flotation material in case your vehicle breaks through the ice over a waterway. Some suits have a flotation device which can be inflated with a few quick puffs. Headgear must include an approved helmet, but avoid the bubble type of face guards as they may frost over. Goggles are a must since they act as sun shields and protect the eyes against snow, cold, tree branches, and other such obstructions. They also protect against snow blindness, and protective lenses can prevent freezing of the eyeballs. Green or grey/brown lenses are recommended for day driving, but clear lenses should be used at night.

A scarf is not recommended for snowmobilers, because the ends may get caught in the machinery. Use a versatile neck-gaiter which will serve a variety of uses. For handwarmers, mittens are the warmest. Gloves or mittens should not fit tightly nor have a shell that gets stiff when cold. Insulated ski gloves are preferred by some and are fine if you find them comfortable. However, you should always carry an extra pair of mittens. A light inner glove or liner prevents freezing of the skin if you must remove outer mittens to handle small items.

Your feet need high-bulk wool or fleece socks worn in a good boot. It is always a good idea to have an extra pair on any trip far from home. Be sure your socks do not create a too tight fit that will cut off circulation—a common cause of cold feet. Boots and socks must keep your feet warm and dry even though you do little walking. Rubber bottomed boots with felt liners and moon boots are popular with snowmobilers.

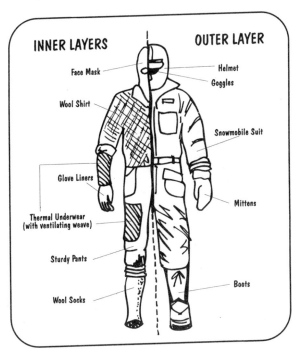

Safety Equipment

Safety and emergency equipment recommendations vary with the terrain and the mileage of your intended trip. Always keep your operator's manual and pre-gapped spark plugs in a handy compartment. Bear in mind that it can take a full day's walk to cover the distance traveled in one hour on the snowmobile. Every snowmobiler should carry these basic tools in the event of a mechanical failure:

• Screwdrivers (including a Phillips) and locking pliers
• Adjustable wrench
• Black electrical tape
• Set of open end wrenches

Also prepare for an emergency. Provide for a return on foot from a disabled machine.

• Map and compass
• First aid kit
• 100 feet of nylon rope (1/4 inch or more)
• Waterproof matches
• High energy foods (at least a one day supply of provisions)
• A pair of snowshoes
• Flashlight and extra batteries
• Flares
• Emergency shelter (tube tent, tarp)
• Space blanket and/or emergency blanket
• Sunblock cream (SPF 30 or above)
• Duct tape
• Expanded tool kit (including special wrenches and a spark plug socket)
• Fuel hose (long enough to be used as a siphon)
• Knife/ax

For added safety, you should also consider some extra items such as a camp stove, fuel, a one-quart pot, and a radio (for storm warnings). If a fire is required, you can use fuel and/or oil drained from your snowmobile to aid in igniting wet wood. If your matches are wet, it is possible to start a fire using your snowmobile's ignition system. Remove a spark plug, re-attach the plug wire to the plug, ground the plug against the snowmobile, crank the engine, and a spark will be created. Use extreme caution to prevent an unmanageable fire.

If your snowmobile breaks down completely, follow the STOP procedures outlined earlier. Remember that your snowmobile, if properly situated, may serve as a shelter or a windbreak.

Cold Water Exposure

Snowmobiling on and around frozen water is possible with proper knowledge and precautions; without them, a frigid dunking can prove fatal. Specialists in physiology have determined the following "safe" immersion times for the unprotected human body:

Water Temperature

At 40 degrees or lower .... Less than 10 minutes
40-50 degrees .... 5 to 20 minutes
50-60 degrees .... 40 minutes
Above 60 degrees .... 1 hour or more

Beyond these limits even a well-conditioned athlete will soon lose all ability to cling to anything for support and rescue must depend completely upon others.

If such a rescue should be necessary, the victim's wet clothing should be removed immediately and the person should be "sandwiched" between two dry companions who have also disrobed. Any available blankets or clothing should then be wrapped around all three people. This massive application of warmth to a great part of a victim's body is the only protection against the phenomenon known as "after cooling" when the constricted outer blood vessels relax in the first relief from frigid water and permit supercooled blood to flow back to the heart, sometimes causing it to fail. Other rescuers should, meanwhile, prepare a fire for warmth and hot beverages but, because of timing, this step is secondary.

Proper dress can eliminate the need for emergency measures. Wool and some synthetic clothes are preferred to other fabrics since they provide some insulation even when wet. A complete change of dry clothing in a waterproof pack is a good safety precaution. However, the best protection is provided by a wetsuit. The style and thickness should be determined by the degree of protection desired.

Since there is considerable heat loss from the top of the head, a wool cap or fleece balaclava should be worn under the helmet. Helmets offer additional protection.

Winter Hazards

For avalanche, hypothermia, frostbite and other winter emergencies, see chapter 4 on winter hazards. Snowmobile safe routes are the same as those for snowshoers and skiers, but snowmobilers must be particularly careful in avalanche country because of the weight and sound level of the machines. Do not drive across the lower parts of slopes and never drive across long open slopes or known avalanche paths. If you are caught in an avalanche, get away from your machine as soon as possible and follow the avalanche instructions given earlier.

Snowmobile Safety Code

1. Bring your snowmobile to top mechanical condition at the beginning of the winter season and throughout the months of use.

2. Familiarize yourself thoroughly with the operator's manual.

3. Wear protective clothing designed specifically for snowmobiling.

4. Use a full size helmet, goggles, or face shield to prevent injuries from twigs, stones, ice chips, and flying debris.

5. Shun long scarves. They may get caught in the moving parts of the snowmobile. (Remember Ruth St. Denis)

6. Know the terrain you plan to ride, particularly the ice and snow conditions. If unfamiliar, consult an area veteran.

7. Heed the weather forecast. Keep a weather eye out and be prepared to beat a retreat at the first sign of dirty weather.

8. Always use the buddy system. Never ride solo.

9. Drowning is a rising cause of snowmobile fatalities. Avoid waterways unless you are 100% familiar with the ice and water currents.

10. Leave the factory-installed air box or muffler intact. A higher decibel muffler will lessen the performance of your vehicle, and add disagreeable racket to the wilderness.

Snowmobile Code of Ethics

1. Do not litter trails or camping areas. Do not pollute streams or lakes.

2. Do not damage living trees, shrubs, or other natural features. Do go out only when there is sufficient snow so that you will not damage the land.

3. Do respect other people's property and rights.

4. Do lend a helping hand when you see someone in distress.

5. Do make your vehicle available to assist in search and rescue parties.

6. Do not interfere with or harass hikers, skiers, snow-shoers, ice anglers, or other winter sports enthusiasts. Do respect their rights to enjoy our recreation facilities.

7. Do know and obey all federal, state, and local rules regulating the operation of snowmobiles in areas where you use your vehicle. Do inform public officials when using public lands.

8. Do not harass wildlife. Avoid areas posted for the protection or feeding of wildlife.

9. Do stay on marked trails or marked roads open to snowmobiles. Do not snowmobile where prohibited.

Snowmobile Trail Signs

When riding your snowmobile, you will encounter trail signs. They are designed to communicate information about the trail to you. Below are some of the most common trail signs for you to learn.

REGULATORY

STOP SIGN
PURPOSE: To be used along trails prior to a road crossing.
SIZE: 12"x12"
BACKGROUND COLOR: Red
BORDER AND LEGEND: Silver

STOP AHEAD SIGN
PURPOSE: To indicate the snowmobiler must stop ahead.
BACKGROUND COLOR AND LEGEND: Yellow with black lettering

TRAILHEAD MARKER
PURPOSE: To indicate snowmobile trailheads and other areas permitting snowmobiling.
BACKGROUND COLOR AND LEGEND: Brown with white border and white snowmobile symbol

RESTRICTIVE
PURPOSE: To indicate areas where snowmobiling is not permitted.
BACKGROUND COLOR AND LEGEND: Brown with white border and white snowmobile symbol with red diagonal stripe

WARNING

TRAIL INTERSECTION
PURPOSE: To indicate an intersection in the trail.
SIZE: 12"x12"
BACKGROUND COLOR: Yellow
LEGEND: Black 2"x11" vertical and 2"x5¹/₄" diagonal

DANGER
PURPOSE: To indicate an area of danger on the snowmobile trail.
SIZE: 12"x12"
BACKGROUND COLOR: Yellow
LEGEND: Black

INFORMATION

TRAIL BLAZER
PURPOSE: Shows snowmobiler is still on the trail.
SIZE: 5"x7"
BACKGROUND COLOR: Orange with reflective border.

DIRECTIONAL BLAZER
PURPOSE: To indicate changes in trail direction.
SIZE: 9¹/₄"x12"
BACKGROUND COLOR: Orange with black border.
LEGEND: Black 5¹/₄" directional arrow

Ski areas are for skiers. Snowmobile traffic ruins cross-country ski tracks. Respect areas marked with ski signs or blue diamonds. These are cross-country ski trails.

6

Winter Camping Safety

Backpacking and wilderness camping are now year-round sports. Snow camping carries some extra rigors, but the compensations—the serenity of the winter wilderness, the magnificence of the skies, and the beauty of the white clad mountain ranges—more than balance out the minor hardships. Like all other winter sports, training and thoughtful preparation reduce the possibility of emergent problems and will add significantly to the pleasures of cold weather camping.

Prior to a first outing, attend one of the winter camping clinics or classes which are provided by many outdoor environmental organizations like the Sierra Club or outdoor retailers such as REI. On your initial outings, travel with experienced snow camp leaders, and go with a minimum group of four (in an emergency, one or two hikers can stay with the victim, the others to return to the trailhead for help).

Additional time in the wilderness multiplies the possibilities of winter hazard occurrences. Snow campers should be particularly knowledgeable about avalanches, hypothermia, and frostbite. It is wise to carry a brochure on the prevention and cure of winter illnesses to refresh one's memory and to share with other campers.

Clothing is particularly important for the winter camper. The recommendations of the clothing chapter above are particularly relevant for campers, but it is advisable to carry a second set of gloves, hat, socks, and neck gaiter to provide insurance for any wet period emergency.

Food is also a critical factor. You should eat considerably more on winter outings (than on summer treks) for you will burn far more calories on cold weather hikes. Take more food and the extra fuel required for the added cooking chores. The additional fuel is particularly necessary to convert snow to water (a bucket of snow makes a cup of water) for cooking and drinking. Water is crucial, since dehydration can lead to hypothermia and altitude sickness. Sip frequently while on the march and in camp. You should average about four quarts a day.

The gear list shown earlier will suffice for snow camping except that the group should carry two stoves and/or spare stove parts and additional ski or snowshoe (whichever is used) straps, bindings, and cables. The tent will also require snow flukes as anchors. One item not previously mentioned but particularly useful for winter camps is a large, large-mouthed, sealable plastic container to serve as a pee-pot in the tent for middle of the night urges.

Despite what you may have heard or read elsewhere, do not cook in your tent. In harsh weather, you can utilize your tent vestibule, an improvised shelter under a plastic sheet or garbage bags, or a windbreaking snow wall constructed just outside the tent vestibule.

Carry two sleeping pads for real comfort, at least one of which should be a closed-cell foam pad. And the nights are long, so bring a good headlamp, extra batteries and emergency reading materials (crossword puzzles or solitaire paper and pencil games if you are a puzzle buff). Keep your day clothes in your sleeping bag, even your boots (in plastic covers) may spend the night at the foot of your bag.

Locate your camp at least 200 feet from any natural water source even if it is frozen or snow covered, and wash and toilet at least 200 feet from that source. If you do not intend to carry out your solid waste in plastic bags, be sure to bury feces in the snow. Carry out used toilet paper as well as any sanitary napkins or tampons. Double plastic bags, individually sealed serve for that purpose.

First Aid Safety

If the occasion to apply first aid arises, remember that "Good Samaritan" laws were enacted by various states to encourage individuals to provide emergency assistance. Those laws are designed to provide legal protection to persons who provide such aid. The laws accept the fact that individuals should do their best to prevent additional injury, or even to save life. In applying first aid, simply use good sense and do not try to exceed your training or your level of ability. You may wish to check your state's "Good Samaritan" legislation.

If the patient is bleeding, try to avoid contact with the blood (or any other body fluid). Use latex gloves, but if they are not available, place a clean cloth between the wound and your hands. If you have any scratches, cuts, or open wounds, be sure to cover those areas with some sort of protective clothing. Wash your hands thoroughly, with soap immediately after providing emergency care. Never touch your mouth, nose, or eyes when giving first aid, nor any clothing or other articles contaminated with blood or body fluids.

Before applying any emergency treatment, the assistance participants should first assess any possible dangers in the area. May the rescuers approach in safety (to themselves and the victim)? Is there avalanche potential? How many members of the party should go forward? Is the slope stable? A quick but reliable assessment of the area is a necessary first step. If the area is deemed safe, proceed to the victim and provide assistance.

RESCUE BREATHING/CPR
Do what the victim ISN'T!
IF NOT BREATHING, BREATHE FOR THEM.
IF NO PULSE, DO CPR.

Skin Protection

Sunscreens

The skin, the largest organ of the body, performs dozens of vital functions, but many winter recreationists neglect skin protection, unaware that skin cancer strikes more than 800,000 Americans each year, winter and summer sports people alike. Winter recreationists must be particularly mindful, for the cold weather evokes an attitude of apathy, but the sun is out in force in the winter, and its effects may be multiplied by reflection off the unending fields of snow and ice.

The medical profession has known for some years that sunlight contains both ultraviolet-B and ultraviolet-A rays, but for an equally long time protection efforts have been aimed only at UVB, the rays that cause burning and cancer. However, it is now known that UVA causes undesirable cosmetic skin changes (wrinkling, discoloration, loss of elasticity) and possibly cancer as well. In response, some sunscreen producers now label their products as "total," "full spectrum," or, specifically, "effective against UVB and UVA rays," despite the fact that the sun protection factor refers only to UVB. There may be some partial truth to those claims, for some companies have added Parsol 1789 (avobenzene) to their lotions, an ingredient which offers some UVA protection. Look for it on the ingredient's label.

Currently, medical recommendations for protection against UVB and UVA is to apply a "full" cover cream with a SPF of 30 or above, and to apply it liberally. Two further sunscreen notes: 1) several prescription and non-prescription drugs can multiply skin sensitivity to sun rays. If you are taking any drugs regularly, use even greater dollops of sun block lotion and apply it more frequently. 2) Last year's sunscreen cream should still be effective (unless it has passed the expiration date shown on some labels). Protective creams should remain effective for three years, but if your lotion or cream is runny or malodorous, give it the deep six.

Insect Repellents

It is unlikely that winter recreationists will be troubled by insects, but since this work recommends erring on the side of caution and safety—this additional note on skin protection.

Since it was first synthesized in a Department of Agriculture laboratory in the early 1950s, N, N-diethyl-meta-toluamide, known as Deet around the world, has ruled the insect repellent roost. (It was approved for consumer use in 1954.) Despite many claims to the contrary, no other product has been proven effective in clinical tests, and no other product compares with Deet in the field.

However, in 1985, three reported deaths among very young girls and some neurological seizures in other children were attributed to Deet and the alarm was sounded. In some regions, Deet concentrations were controlled and in one state, Deet was banned totally (now repealed). In response, some medical researchers and the Deet producers pointed to the staggering statistical safety records of Deet—used by more than 100 million people each year with fewer than ten reports (average) of adverse side effects, mostly on repeated use on children—a medical and manufacturer's prohibition. Many doctors now conclude that Deet used in accordance with the manufacturer's instructions, is a safe chemical product. Nonetheless, the decision to use Deet remains a strictly personal option.

The current recommendation is to use Deet in concentrations of 40% or less (less than 20% for children), and to use it sparingly, reapplying only as needed. Do not apply the lotion near the eyes, on lips, or on broken skin. Control the application (finger application is better than a spray), apply it as a thin layer, and do not rub it in. If you are applying skin cream or sunblock separately, put them on first and the Deet lotion last. Do not apply Deet to underclothes (particularly child's underwear), but spray or apply lightly to outer clothes. Be aware, however, that Deet may damage rayon, acetate, or Spandex. Twenty-five percent Deet works well, but it must be applied more frequently.

Those recreationists who elect an alternative to Deet will find those lotions may now be labeled "repellents" (by law). Citronella, a naturally derived oil of an Asian grass is toxic above 10% and was banned formerly. Today's permissible higher concentration levels have yet to be tested for effective repellency, but concentrations decreasing below 10% show a concomitant weakening potency.

Buyers of Deet products should be aware that they are paying for the Deet, and not for the inexpensive inert carrying lotion or cream. A 5% Deet lotion should not cost more than a 40% equivalent size product. That caveat does not apply if the Deet is packaged with sunblock lotion, or a sunblock and skin conditioner cream all in one—as is increasingly the current mode. Finally, one may still buy inexpensive bottles of 100% Deet (many hikers were using such concentrations which were sold as army surplus after World War II), which may be cut to an appropriate concentration with skin lotion and repackaged in a small plastic squeeze bottle.

Eye Protection

Sunglasses are essential for winter sports people. Ultraviolet and intense sunlight are the enemies, and account for eye degeneration and cataract development as well as painful short-term keratitis, snow blindness. Up to 100,000 of the million cataract cases reported annually in the U.S. may be sun-related. Mountain people are at even greater risk, for UVB rays, the worse of the ultraviolet, are twice as damaging at 10,000 feet as they are at sea level. The answer is a good pair of sunglasses.

In few products, however, is high style as costly as it is in sunglasses. Buying for style is a personal decision (as long as the style, such as mini lenses, does not conflict with protection), but be sure to buy for quality. Good sunglasses are now classified: "Cosmetic" (blocks 70% of UVB, 20% of UVA, and up to 60% of visible light), "General Purpose" (blocks 95% of UVB, 60% of UVA, and up to 90% of visible light), and "Special Purpose" (blocks at least 99% of UVB, 60% of UVA, and up to 97% of visible light). Snow people should purchase "Special Purpose" glasses whose tag reads "absorbs UV up to 400 nm." Such a tag indicates complete absorption of UVA and UVB rays.

Sunglasses should have sturdy frames with as scratchproof a surface and as shatterproof a lens as possible. A choice between those recommendations may be required because plastic lenses, though lighter in weight and practically shatterproof, are prone to scratches while glass lenses resist scratches but are more easily shattered.

People out in the mountain snow all day should probably opt for glacier glasses, featuring the darkest tint lenses, which block about 95% of the visible light, and side shields, leather triangles which help to bar the intense light from the sides. Such glasses may not serve well at lower altitudes and specifically not for driving or even the beach or the desert in summer. Lighter tint glasses are appropriate for those occasions.

In an emergency (lost, stolen, or forgotten glasses) you can do well with an inexpensive pair of substitute specs whose tag indicates a high percentage of UV filtration, whose frames are strong, and whose lenses do not show distortion. (Hold the glasses at arm's length and peer through each lens with a single eye focusing on right angle vertical and horizontal lines in the store. Move the lenses slightly. If the lines remain straight, the lenses are okay.)

Color tints are personal matters, though dark gray is generally recommended for snow outings. Gray and green are the most popular tints and are least likely to distort colors. Brown, amber and yellow colors tend to enhance contrasts. Colors such as red, blue and purple tend to distort colors excessively and are not recommended. Whatever your choice, be certain to wear your glasses.

A very useful complement to the glasses is a broad-brimmed hat which will shade the eyes throughout the day. Many snow trekkers would as soon do without their sunspecs, as they would a brimmed hat. Too hot for a hat? Wear a strap-on, tie-on or snap-on visor. In snow, wear your hat.

Leave No Trace

Leave No Trace is a set of ethical principles and associated educational programs designed to protect and conserve outdoor recreation areas particularly backcountry and wilderness regions. The programs hope to raise public awareness of the need for such protections. For further information, contact Leave No Trace Inc., P.O. Box 997, Boulder, CO 80306. Phone: 1-800-332-4100, http://www.lnt.org.

Principles of Leave No Trace

Plan Ahead and Prepare
- Know the regulations and special concerns of the area you'll visit.
- Visit the backcountry in small groups.
- Avoid popular areas during peak-use periods.
- Choose equipment and clothing in subdued colors.
- Repack all food in plastic bags, self-knotted for closure (no twisties or rubber bands). Never take glass into the backcountry.

Camp and Travel on Durable Surfaces
On the trail:
• Stay on designated trails. Walk single file in the middle of the path.

• Stay on the trail on switchbacks. Never use shortcuts.

• When traveling cross-country, choose the most durable surfaces available, such as rock, gravel, dry grasses, or snow. Spread the group. Do not hike single file.

• Use a map and compass to eliminate the need for rock cairns, tree scars and ribbons. Keep the wilderness wild.

• If you encounter pack animals, step to the downhill side of the trail and speak softly to avoid startling them.

• If you stop to rest, move well off the trail, and sit and keep your pack on a durable surface.

At camp:
• Choose an established, legal site that will not be damaged by your stay. If possible, use a heavily-impacted site. Reject any area showing early signs of impact.

• Restrict activities to areas where vegetation is compacted or absent.

• Keep pollutants out of the water by camping at least 200 feet (about 70 adult steps) from lakes and streams.

Pack It In and Pack It Out
• Take everything you bring into the wild back out with you.

• Protect wildlife and your food by storing provisions securely.

• Pick up all spilled foods.

Properly Dispose of What You Can't Pack Out
• Deposit human waste in six-by-eight-inch deep catholes at least 200 feet from water, camps, or trails.

Cover and disguise the catholes when you're finished.

- Use toilet paper or wipes sparingly; pack them out, or use natural substitutes such as leaves, smooth stones or sticks, snow, etc. Deposit these substitutes in the cathole.
- To wash your dishes, carry the water 200 feet from any stream or lake and scrub the dishes clean (no soap). Rinse with boiling water. Strain the dishwater, deposit the food scraps in the garbage to be carried out and scatter the gray-water over a wide area. Always minimize the use of soap. To wash your body, handscrub with no soap while swimming or wading. Wash your hands in a basin 200 feet from any water source. Use minimal soap only after toileting or before meal preparation.
- Inspect your campsite for trash and evidence of your stay. Pack out all trash—both yours and others!

Leave What You Find

- Treat our natural heritage with respect. Leave plants, rocks, and historical artifacts as you found them.
- Good campsites are found, not made. Do not alter a campsite.
- Let nature's sounds prevail; keep loud voices and noises to a minimum.
- Leave pets at home. If you must take a dog along, keep it under strict control at all times and remove its feces.
- Do not build structures or furniture or dig trenches. Never carry nails, a hammer, an axe or a saw.

Minimize Use and Impact of Fire

- Campfires can have a lasting impact on the backcountry. Always carry a lightweight stove for cooking, and use a candle lantern instead of a fire whenever possible.

- Where fires are permitted, use established fire rings, fire pans, or mound fires only. Do not scar large rocks or overhangs.
- Gather firewood sticks no larger than an adult's wrist. Gather widely. Do not deplete any area.
- Do not snap branches off live, dead, or downed trees.
- Extinguish campfires totally.
- Remove all unburned trash from the ring for disposal at the trailhead. Burn the wood to a white ash and scatter the cold ashes over a large area well away from any camp.

In Arid Areas

- Conserve and use water judiciously.
- Carry your drinking and cooking water if possible.
- Small water holes mean survival for desert creatures. Respect that need. Never bathe or swim in small pools.
- Use small water pockets for drinking only. Dip into the pocket with a clean cup.

Further Reading

Avalanche

*1. Armstrong, Betsy R., and Williams, Knox. *The Avalanche Book.* Revised and updated. Fulcrum Publishing; Golden, Colorado: 1992.

2. Fredston, Jill A., and Fesler, Doug. *Snow Sense: A Guide to Evaluating Snow Avalanche Hazard.* Revised Ed. Alaska Mountain Safety Center Inc.; Anchorage, Alaska: 1994.

3. McClung, David, and Schaerer, Peter. *The Avalanche Handbook.* 2nd Ed. The Mountaineers; Seattle, Washington: 1993.

4. LaChapelle, E.R. *The ABC of Avalanche Safety.* 2nd Ed. The Mountaineers; Seattle, Washington: 1985. (Booklet)

First Aid

5. Goth, Peter, and Isaac, Jeff. *The Outward Bound Wilderness First-Aid Handbook.* Lyons and Burford; New York, New York: 1991.

6. Lentz, Martha J.; Macdonald, Steven C.; and Carline, Jan D. *Mountaineering First Aid: A Guide to Accident Response & First Aid Care.* 4th Ed. The Mountaineers; Seattle Washington: 1996.

*7. Schimelpfenig, Tod, and Lindsey, Linda. *NOLS Wilderness First Aid.* The National Outdoor Leadership School; Lander, Wyoming, and Stackpole Books; Mechanicsburg, Pennsylvania: 1991.

8. Tilton, Buck. *Backcountry First Aid and Extended Care.* 2nd Ed. ICS Books; Merrillville, Indiana: 1994. (Booklet)

9. Weiss, Eric A. *A Comprehensive Guide to Wilderness and Travel Medicine.* Adventure Medical Kits; Oakland, California: 1992. (Booklet)

---

* = **Recommended**

Mountain Medicine
Hypothermia, Frostbite, Altitude Sickness

10. Bezruchka, Stephen. *Altitude Illness: Prevention and Treatment.* The Mountaineers; Seattle, Washington: 1994. (Booklet)
11. Darvill, Fred T. Jr. *Mountaineering Medicine: A Wilderness Medical Guide.* 13th Ed. Wilderness Press; Berkeley, California: 1992.
12. Forgey, William W. *The Basic Essentials of Hypothermia.* ICS Books Inc.; Merrillville, Indiana: 1991.
13. Forgey, William W. Ed. *Wilderness Medical Society—Practice Guidelines for Wilderness Emergency Care.* ICS Books Inc.; Merrillville, Indiana: 1995. (Booklet)
*14. Forgey William W. *Wilderness Medicine Beyond First Aid.* 4th Ed. ICS Books Inc.; Merrillville, Indiana: 1994.
15. Wilkerson, James A. Ed; Banz, Cameron C; and Hayward, John S. *Hypothermia, Frostbite and Other Cold Injuries: Preventing Recognition, Pre Hospital Treatment.* The Mountaineers; Seattle, Washington: 1986. (Booklet)
*16. Wilkerson, James A. Ed. *Medicine for Mountaineering & Other Wilderness Activities.* 4th Ed. The Mountaineers; Seattle, Washington: 1992.

Winter Sports

17. Bennett, Jeff. *The Complete Snowboarder.* McGraw Hill Companies; New York, New York: 1994.
18. Curtis, Sam. *Harsh Weather Camping.* 2nd Ed. Menasha Ridge Press; Birmingham, Alabama: 1993.
*19. Edwards, Sally and McKenzie, Melissa. *Snowshoeing.* Human Kinetics; Champaign, Illinois: 1995.
20. Gamma, Karl. *The Handbook of Skiing.* Revised Ed. Alfred A. Knopf Company; New York, New York: 1992.
21. Gullion Lurie. *Nordic Skiing: Steps to Success.* Human Kinetics; Champaign, Illinois: 1993.
*22. Lowe, Jeff. *Ice World: Techniques and Experiences of Modern Ice Climbing.* The Mountaineers; Seattle, Washington: 1996.
23. Poster, Carol. *The Basic Essentials of Alpine Skiing.* ICS Books Inc.; Merrillville, Indiana: 1993.
24. Prater, Gene. *Snow-Shoeing.* 3rd Ed. The Mountaineers; Seattle, Washington: 1988.
25. Raleigh, Duane. *Ice: Tools and Technique.* Elk Mountain Press; Carbondale, Colorado: 1995.
26. Reichenfeld, Rob, and Bruechert, Anna. *Snowboarding.* Human Kinetics; Champaign, Illinois: 1995.
27. Stark, Peter, and Krauzer, Steven, M. *Winter Adventure: A Complete Guide to Winter Sports.* W.W. Norton and Company; New York, New York: 1995.
28. Townsend, Chris. *Wilderness Skiing and Winter Camping.* McGraw Hill Companies; New York, New York: 1993.

29. Watters, Ron. *Ski Camping: A Guide to the Delights of Back Country Skiing.* Revised Ed. Great Rift Press; Pocatello, Idaho: 1989.
30. Werner, Doug. *Snowboarders Start Up: A Beginner's Guide to Snowboarding.* Pathfinder Publishing of California; Ventura, California: 1993.

Snowmobile

*31. *Snowmobile Safety and You.* Outdoor Empire Publishing Inc.; Seattle, Washington: 1994. (Write: Washington State Parks and Recreation Commission, 7150 Clearwater Lane, Olympia, Washington 98504-2662, or call (206) 586-0186.)

Leave No Trace— Minimum Impact Camping

*32. Hampton, Bruce, and Cole, David. *Soft Paths: How to Enjoy the Wilderness Without Harming It.* Revised and Updated ed. Stackpole Books; Mechanicsburg, Pennsylvania: 1995. (A National Outdoor Leadership School book.)
33. Harmon, Will. *Wild Country Companion.* Falcon Press; Helena, Montana: 1994.
34. Schatz, Curt, and Seemon, Dan. *Minimum Impact Camping: A Basic Guide.* Adventure Publications; Cambridge, Minnesota: 1994.

Index

by
Teresa L. Jacobsen

Alpine ski safety rules, 56-57
Altitude sickness, 50-51
Automobile, 1-10
    engine care, 2
    safety, 1-3, 10
    see also Driving
Avalanches, 35-43
    danger signs, 39-41
    route selection, 40-41
    snowmobile and, 66
    survival, 41-43
    terrain, 36-38
    types of, 35-36
    weather factors, 38-39

Boots, 13-14

Camping safety, 69-71
Chains, Tire, 4
Clothing, 11-17, 62-63
Code of ethics, snowmobile, 67-68

Dehydration, 49, 70
Distress signals, 53
Driving, 5-10
    in fog, 9
    in rain, 9-10
    in snow and ice, 5-9

Emergencies and accidents,
    falling in water, 65-66
    getting lost, 51-53
    missing party, 53

Equipment,
    camping, 70-71
    winter sports, 19-23
    snowmobile, 64-65
Equivalent Chill Temperature
    (chart), 48
Exercise, 27-28

First aid, 73-74
    cold water exposure, 65-66
    frostbite, 49-50
    hypothermia, 46-47
    kits, 20, 23-26
    training list, 25-26
Fog, 9
Food, 28-30, 70
Frostbite, 49-50

Gaiters, 14, 15, 62-63
Global Positioning System (GPS),
    26-27
Gloves, 12, 15, 17
Goggles, 62
Ground to air signals, 53

Hats, 14-15, 16, 81
Hazards, Winter, 35-53
    altitude sickness, 50-51
    avalanches, 35-43
    dehydration, 49
    falling in water, 65-66
    frostbite, 49-50

hyperventilation, 51
hypothermia, 44-48
ice, 43
lost or late, 51-53
wind chill, 48
Helmets, 62
Hyperventilation, 51
Hypothermia, 44-48
seven steps (chart), 44
symptoms, 45
treatment, 45-48

Ice hazards, 43
Insect repellents, 76-78

Jackets, 16

Leave No Trace, 83-87
Loose snow avalanches, 35
Lost person, 51-53

Neck gaiters, 14, 62-63
Nordic ski safety rules, 54-55
Nutrition, 28-30

Pants, 14, 15-16

Rescue beacons, 42-43

Safety,
backcountry, 53-54
snowmobile, 66-67
Signals, 52-53
Skier's responsibility code, 57

Ski safety rules, 56-57
Slab avalanches, 36
Sledding safety rules, 59-60
Snowboard safety rules, 58-59
Snowmobile, 61-68
clothing, 62-63
code of ethics, 67-68
emergencies, 65-66
equipment, 64-65
safety, 64-65
safety code, 66-67
Snowshoe safety rules, 54-55
Socks, 12, 13
S.T.O.P. System, 51-52
Sunglasses, 79-80
Sunscreen, 75-76
Sweater, 14

Telephones, 26-27
Tire chains, 4
Trail symbols, 56

Underwear, 12

Water,
drinking, 31
falling in, 65-66
purification, 31-34
Wind chill chart, 48
Winter hazards, *see* Hazards
Winterizing, 2-3

Typestyles used:
Chapter Heads: Cooper Black
Text: Bookman Bold, Bookman
Page Numbers: Sans Bold Reversed
Running Heads: Bookman Bold

Printed on recycled paper:
James River 60 lb.
recycled white offset